Swift
An Illustrated Life

Jonathan Swift, by Bindon, engraved by Andrew Miller, 1743. The document reads: 'Q. Anne's Letters Pat.: of the First Fruits & 20th Parts for the Poor Clergy of Ireland Dated 17th Feb: 10th of her Reign'

COMHAIRLE CHONTAE ÁTHA CLIATH THEAS
SOUTH DUBLIN COUNTY LIBRARIES

LUCAN LIBRARY
TO RENEW ANY ITEM TEL:

Items should be returned on or before the last date below. Fines, as displayed in the Library, will be charged on overdue items.

IONATHAN SWIFT S.T.D.
Decanus Ecclesiæ Cathedralis Sancti
Patricij DUBLIN.

Geo. Vertue Londini Sculpsit

Swift
An Illustrated Life

BRUCE ARNOLD

THE LILLIPUT PRESS
DUBLIN

First published 1999 by
THE LILLIPUT PRESS LTD
62–63 Sitric Road, Arbour Hill, Dublin 7, Ireland
e-mail: lilliput@indigo.ie
http://indigo.ie/~lilliput

A CIP record for this title is available from the British Library

ISBN 1 901866 39 4

The Lilliput Press receives financial assistance from
An Chomhairle Ealaíon / The Arts Council of Ireland.

*Frontispiece: Jonathan Swift, engraved by George Vertue, after a
portrait by Charles Jervas. This is a reverse image of the line
engraving by Fourdrinier, and it appears as the frontispiece to the
first volume of* The Works, *printed in Dublin in 1735 in four
volumes by George Faulkner.*

Set in 12.5 on 16 Janson

Printed in Ireland by ColourBooks of Baldoyle, Dublin

Contents

Illustrations

Introduction

For more than three centuries, Jonathan Swift's personality and character have presented problems for those interested in his life and work. He is a man of paradoxes. Despite his love for individuals, he described himself as one who 'hated' mankind; despite his love of fame, he took great pains to ensure that his writings should never carry his name; despite his self-confidence as a writer, in his private life he was often prey to self-doubt.

Swift's capacity for love and friendship was immense. He loved two women, Esther Johnson and Esther Van Homrigh, known to him as Stella and Vanessa, but he loved them in very different ways. Stella became Swift's ward on the death of his patron, Sir William Temple, and remained so for the duration of her life, always accompanied by Rebecca Dingley,

a Temple cousin. Swift's love for Stella was in the character of familial love, approximating to that of an uncle for a favourite niece. He guided and guarded her interests from her childhood to her death, and wrote about her in words that move the heart as much as anything he wrote. With Vanessa he enjoyed a turbulent yet rewarding love affair, which lasted from 1707 until her death in 1723. It is recorded in letters and in his poem *Cadenus and Vanessa*. The unorthodox nature of these relationships should not obscure the natural warmth that suffuses all we know on the subject. On the one hand, Swift's feelings rise at times to a passionate intensity; on the other they amaze us with their detailed concern for a woman's life in all its diversity and tribulation.

Something of the same naturalness is to be found in his friendships with men, some of which were lasting and deep. The traditional conviction about Swift is that he was volatile, argumentative, bitter, disdainful, withering, mocking, and that his underlying instinct was towards anger and confrontation. In a sense this was true. He marked out his path in areas where conflict was inevitable. To be true to himself he had to confront those who sought to obstruct him or the men he served. And he lived in an age when satire was a ready weapon for most writers. Yet this should not overshadow the other side of his character, where warmth and vulnerability are to be found.

A year after the death of Stella, Swift wrote a letter jointly to his friends Viscount Bolingbroke and Alexander Pope. They exemplified the two strands in

Alexander Pope, by Jean Baptiste Van Loo, engraved by John Faber

his life that had mattered most to him, politics and poetry, and they had an understanding of him that was rare in its range and depth. The letter, dated April 1729, not only indicates Swift's warmth of character and depth of feeling, but also offers us a number of other clues to character which are worth pursuing:

I am ashamed to tell you, that when I was very young I had more desire to be famous than ever since; and fame, like all things else in this life, grows with me every day more a trifle ... I hate a crowd where I have not an easy place to see and be seen. A great Library always maketh me melancholy, where the best Author is as much squeezed, and as obscure, as a Porter at a Coronation. ... I tell you it is almost incredible how Opinions change by the decline or decay of spirits, and I will further tell you, that all my endeavours from a boy to distinguish my self, were only for want of a great Title and Fortune, that I might be used like a Lord by those who have an opinion of my parts; whether right or wrong it is no great matter; and so the reputation of wit or learning does the office of a blue riband, or of a coach and six horses. To be remembered for ever on the account of our friendship, is what would exceedingly please me, but yet I never loved to make a visit, or be seen walking with my betters, because they get all the eyes and civility from me. I no sooner writ this than I corrected my self, and remembered Sir Faulk Grevil's Epitaph, 'Here lies Xc. who was friend to Sir Philip Sidney.' ... You must present my humble services to Mrs Pope, and let her know I pray for her continuance in the world, for her own reason, that she may live to take care of you.[1]

There are many layers of thought on display here. Trusted friends are treated with absolute openness on subjects which Swift rarely dealt with at any level. Here we have his youthful desire to be famous and his sense of frustration at not achieving his ambition in the terms he wished. The feelings are expressed in concrete terms. He wants to see and be seen in a crowd. He wants the notice that fame brings, the admiration, the physical recognition. He knows his talent, he knows it is acknowledged by his friends, and yet he walks within a library conscious of the smallness of what he has achieved, and conscious even more of how 'Opinions change by the decline or decay of spirits'.

He was in his early sixties when he wrote these words. *Gulliver's Travels* was already behind him. He was facing old age, limited further prospects as a writer, loss of energy and power. Reading this letter, we are persuaded to cast our eyes forward, into the future which Swift faced, and to experience some of its bleakness. But he also directs our gaze backwards, even as far as his childhood. These words bring us close to the character of Jonathan Swift. They reveal him as a man of great intellect, sensitive in his feelings, bruised by his childhood, embittered by his knowledge of human behaviour, and almost certainly starved of love and affection, perhaps even from the day of his birth, a day which he regularly and relentlessly cursed in the words of the third chapter of the Book of Job.

Detail from map of Dublin by Charles Brooking, 1728, showing view of south side

I

Swift's Upbringing

Jonathan Swift was born in Dublin in 1667. His mother's husband, Jonathan Swift the Elder, had died several months previously, and partly as a consequence of this the identity of Swift's father has been in question since his own lifetime. The most likely candidate is Sir John Temple, Master of the Rolls in Ireland. Swift was to live for ten years in the household of his son, Sir William Temple, a move for which no explanation is wholly satisfactory without consanguinity.

The small walled city of Swift's birth, largely medieval in its streets and buildings, was dominated by Dublin Castle, the administrative centre of Ireland. The members of the extended Swift family were involved in the legal profession, then centred in the vicinity of Christ Church Cathedral. Jonathan Swift the Elder was a clerk in the King's Inns of Court,

Left: *Sir John Temple, by Cornelius Johnson*

Right: *Detail from a view of White-haven, Cumbria, by Matthew Read, engraved by Richard Parr, 1738*

Below: *'A Prospect of the Custom House and Essex Bridge, Dublin', by J. Tudor, engraved by Richard Parr, 1753*

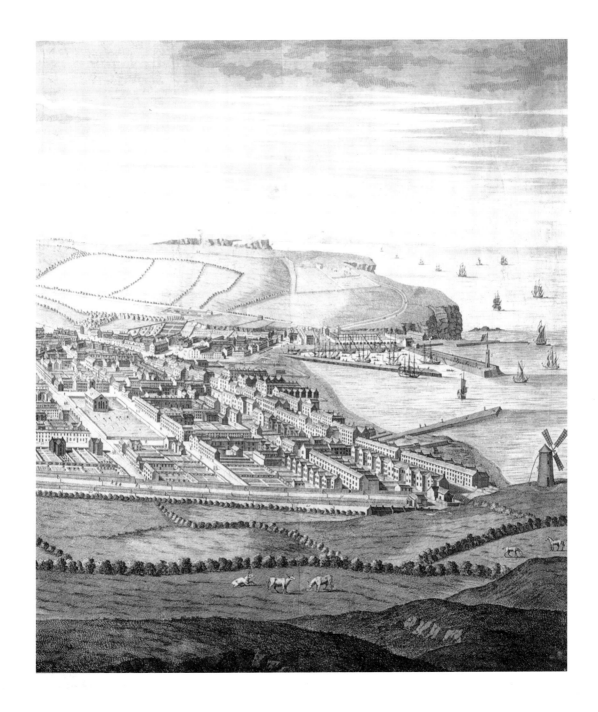

which were located on the north side of the river Liffey, on Inns Quay, roughly where the Four Courts are today. The only bridge across the river was at this point, according to Bernard de Gomme's map of 1673, though other bridges were constructed in the following two decades. The one immediately below Dublin Castle, Essex Bridge, led across the river to the centre of the much smaller areas of commercial activity on the north side. For much of the eighteenth century, Essex Bridge was the last before the open sea; downstream from it the river was crossed by ferries and immediately beside it stood the old Custom House. It was probably from the Custom House Quay that the infant Swift and his nurse, in mysterious circumstances, went aboard the trading vessel that brought them to Whitehaven, on the Cumbrian coast of England. Swift was to spend his first three years there. His mother, meanwhile, removed from Dublin to Leicester, her town of origin, and there is no record of mother and son living together except on later visits which the mature Swift paid to England.

The age into which Swift was born was one of political and constitutional turbulence in both Ireland and England. Swift was born only seven years after the Restoration of Charles II. The return to monarchy brought back a generally liberal regime. Theatres opened again, and women were permitted to act in plays. The King had numerous mistresses and his court was pleasure-loving, though at the same time threatened by European powers, most immediately the Dutch, who dominated trade at sea.

James, Duke of York, and later King James II of England and James VII of Scotland, by Godfrey Kneller, mezzotint by J. Smith

Great issues were fought out in the century of Swift's birth: the rights of monarchy, the strength of the law, the balance of power between central authority and the owners of land throughout the kingdom. But if one single matter remained critical throughout, it was Protestantism: its survival, its shape and character, its strength in politics and therefore in legislation, and its tolerance of diversity, both within its own broad house, and between itself and the Roman Catholic power structure in Europe, which asserted itself so forcefully in the last fifteen years of the century and had so powerful an impact in Ireland.

In England there was a great fear of Roman Catholic influence in high places, including the court. This was reinforced when the conversion to Catholicism of the King's brother James, the Duke of York, was forced into the open, leading to his resignation as Lord High Admiral. James was the likely successor to his brother, and the shadow of his faith hung over the realm. There was no doubt, however, of the underlying strength of Protestantism. In Ireland the situation was different. It was not just 'in high places', as in England, that control over the growth of Roman Catholic power had to be exercised, but throughout the land-owning community. Protestantism had become part of the policing of the territory. Following the Restoration there was some relaxation of this, with confiscated land being given back to Catholics 'loyal' to the Crown, and with the re-assigning of further land to influential Protestants affected by this. But this part of the kingdom remained potentially volatile and a threat to the new-found stability.

The dominant political figure in Ireland at the time of Swift's birth was the first Duke of Ormonde, 'The Great Duke'. Born in London, the son of Lord Thurles and grandson of the eleventh Earl of Ormonde, in 1632 he succeeded to the earldom. Soon after the rebellion of 1641 he was appointed commander-in-chief of the army in Ireland, and spent much of the next six years fighting first the Irish and later the Parliamentary forces. He was appointed Lord Lieutenant in 1643, and Chancellor of Trinity College in 1645. In 1647 he was compelled by Parliamentary pressure to leave Ireland; he returned the following year, but his defeat at the Battle of Rathmines drove him out again, and he followed Charles II to France in 1650. After the Restoration he was

James Butler, first Duke of Ormonde, by David Loggan, engraved by M. Van der Gucht

raised to the dukedom and resumed the office of Lord Lieutenant, which he held until 1669 and again from 1677 to 1685. He was widely respected for his strength and good looks, his dignified presence, his personal integrity and his unswerving loyalty to the throne.

Ormonde's ancestor, the eighth Earl of Ormonde, had founded the Kilkenny School, which Swift attended. Swift appears to have been in the wardship of his uncle Godwin Swift, a Dublin lawyer, who had a large family of his own, but seems to have had funds available to send Swift to school and university. The school term was essentially year-long, with short breaks at Easter, Whitsuntide and Christmas, possibly permitting Swift to travel occasionally to Dublin, but in reality confining his experience for this period to the gracious and prosperous town a hundred miles south-west of the capital. The school was reputedly expensive, though alternative views have been offered about this, and also about both its quality and standing. Surviving information, even that of Swift himself, leaves it unclear as to who decided on his education at Kilkenny School, and who paid for it. The same question arises over his attendance of Trinity College. In the late seventeenth century these two institutions were attended by well-to-do Protestants. But Jonathan Swift was not well-to-do.

Swift overlapped at school with William Congreve, three years his junior, whom he later knew in London. His Masters at the school were Edward Jones and Henry Ryder. Both were Cambridge men, and had been at Westminster School. They belonged firmly to the Calvinist tradition, and their teaching would have shaped Swift's own Christian upbringing. Each went on to become a bishop in the Church of Ireland: Jones was Bishop of Cloyne and Ryder was Bishop of Killaloe.

There was both an Ormonde and a Calvinist association between Kilkenny College and Trinity College. The Duke of Ormonde watched over both institutions paternalistically, and in the case of the school he literally looked down on it from the windows of his castle in Kilkenny. He saw as natural the transition from the school to the university, which he regarded in turn as a 'nursery for clergymen' whose destiny it would be to staff the parishes of the Church of Ireland. The religious training in the Kilkenny

School was similar in its traditions to Cambridge, where Puritan belief was strong through the seventeenth century.

Trinity College, when Swift entered it in April 1682, was well to the east of the centre of Dublin and essentially medieval in appearance, its buildings quite low and its layout dominated by the spire of an earlier Augustinian priory, which was a beacon for shipping coming up the Liffey. A series of formal squares was surrounded by unbroken low-roofed structures which included staff and student accommodation, and earlier buildings, none of which now survive, housed the library, chapel and examination hall, and the provost's residence. Its setting was largely rural. There was reclaimed land north as far as the Liffey, but this was undeveloped. The old St Andrew's Church, beside the Castle, had been demolished, and a new church, round and castellated in the style of the Templar churches in London and elsewhere, had been constructed on its present site; it was the only significant building between the College and the top end of Dame Street. St Stephen's Green, to the south, was laid out, walled and ditched for protection, and those properties facing onto the enclosed green obtained by ballot, which led initially to buildings on the two sides nearest to the city. During the next forty years, as a result of a pincer movement of development, the College was embraced by the city and became an important focus of activity.

The significant people in Swift's life at the time included his tutor, St George Ashe (1658–1718). A native of County Roscommon, Ashe graduated from Trinity College in 1676 and was elected Fellow three years later. His particular interest was in mathematics and experimental philosophy, and he became Professor of Mathematics. In a paper read in the early 1680s to the Dublin Philosophical Society, he argued in favour of the supreme value of mathematical study, 'because quantity, the object about which it is conversant, is a sensible obvious thing, and consequently the ideas we form thereof are clear and distinct and daily represented to us in most familiar instances'.[2]

As a member of the Dublin Philosophical Society he was a friend of William Molyneux, whom he succeeded as secretary. Thanks to Molyneux's friendship with John Locke, Ashe was in close touch with the latest ideas in philosophy, science and mathematics. Several decades later this found expression in the undergraduate course at Trinity, and was of great value to graduate students and fellowship candidates, including George Berkeley (1685–1753). Ashe became Bishop of Cloyne in 1695; he was translated to Clogher in 1697, and to Derry in 1717. But he always remained in close touch with Dublin University, and from 1702 to 1713 he was Vice-Chancellor. In 1692, when Trinity College was still recovering from the Jacobite occupation, he was appointed Provost. Although he held the post for less than three years, he had an important influence on the College's intellectual atmosphere.

Swift of course came under the influence of many others during his time at Trinity College. There were two Provosts during his period there, Narcissus Marsh and Robert Huntington.

Narcissus Marsh (1638–1713), born in Wiltshire, was appointed Provost of Dublin University in 1679 with the backing of the Duke of Ormonde. He then became Bishop of Ferns, around 1683, and afterwards held in succession three archbishoprics, Cashel (1691–4), Dublin (1694–1703) and Armagh (1703–13). His enduring claim to fame was the magnificent library he assembled and left to the city of Dublin. Situated in its own building close to the Deanery of St Patrick's, it became the main library consulted by Swift after his return from London in 1714 to take up the post of Dean.

Marsh disliked being Provost, finding the university 'very troublesome' because of administrative duties and the 'rude and ignorant' students: 'I was quickly weary of 340 young men and boys in this lewd and debauch'd town.'[3] Swift loathed Marsh. His vituperative attack dates from many years later, and Irvin Ehrenpreis, quoting it, says it 'might suggest a reaction against an adolescent awe of apparent saintliness and erudition'. But Marsh was of value and interest to Swift, in teaching him something of logic, and also, more indirectly, by being one of the founding figures of the Dublin Philosophical Society, along with William Petty and William Molyneux.[4]

Robert Huntington (1637–1701), Marsh's successor as Provost, was also involved with the Society, the first formal meeting of which took place in his lodgings in 1684. To it he gave support, and made a modest philosophical contribution. He seems not to have influenced Swift in any way that called forth retrospective criticism. His involvement with Ireland was slight; he took the appointment reluctantly, stayed until the general flight of Protestants began in 1688, and then remained in England apart from brief visits, giving up the provostship in 1692, when he was replaced by St George Ashe.

Swift's studies at Trinity College were greatly reinforced by his familiarity with the scholarly pursuits of the Dublin Philosophical Society. The two institutions represent the twin poles of his later education in Dublin. It is easy today to stress the absurdities with which individual members of the Society became involved. These furnished Swift with material to be included in his *A Tale of a Tub*, and in the third part of *Gulliver's Travels*. But the members of the Society were seriously concerned with two absolutes of scientific research, unresolved to this day: how life began, and how the brain works. It would be wrong to suggest that the youthful Swift, still a student, would have treated either their scientific investigations, or their parallel teaching practices in the university, with intellectual disdain. Swift's later satire was of a different scale and origin, and there is no evidence whatever that at this point in his life he was dismissive towards the curious, even extraordinary experiments and investigations pursued by these Society members.

Trinity College taught Swift language, logic, theology, mathematics, science, philosophy. His later reaction against many of those involved in his teaching, including Narcissus Marsh, should not be read back into his time as a student. We know enough of this to recognize normal recalcitrance, indifferent performance, waywardness and indolence, but no more.

Sir William Temple, by Sir Peter Lely, engraved by T.A. Dean

II

Moor Park

His formal education over, Swift's real education in the world of politics and literature began.

Swift left Trinity and Ireland early in 1689. He gave as his reason 'the Troubles then breaking out',[5] and this is endorsed by Sir William Temple, who claimed that Swift 'was forced away by the desertion of that College upon the calamities of the country'.[6] On its own the move from Ireland would have been of little value, taking him from immediate danger into what was only comparative safety in England. There has never been an adequate explanation of the circumstances under which, after time spent with his mother, near Leicester, he joined the household of Sir William Temple (1628–99), at Moor Park, near Farnham in Surrey. The explanation generally given derives from Swift's supposed assertion, as reported by his cousin Deane Swift, that his mother advised her son to go to Temple:

I really cannot tell you in your present circumstances what advice to give you, but suppose you would apply yourself to Sir WILLIAM TEMPLE, who is both a great and a wise man? I cannot but think he would at least give you some directions, and perhaps, if he were acquainted with your uncomfortable situation, recommend you to some kind of employment either in church or state. His lady you know is a relation of ours, and besides his father, Sir JOHN TEMPLE had a regard and friendship for your father and for your uncles until his last hour. Go your ways in the name of GOD to Sir WILLIAM TEMPLE, and upon asking his advice you will immediately perceive what encouragement or preferment you are likely to expect from his friendship.[7]

This was the single most important event in his life, and Sir William Temple himself the single greatest influence over him. Temple endowed and trained Swift as both a man and a writer, giving him a wealth of intellectual, moral and social understanding. Temple himself was a notable example of moral purpose in an age when this seemed to be in a state of disintegration in the face of intellectual inquiry. His achievements as a statesman and diplomat had been substantial. His output as a writer, in which Swift in time was to play a part, was already impressive. And there was the added appeal that Temple had withdrawn from the world he had served and was living, like a retired consul or senator of classical times, in a fine house surrounded by gardens and parklands, setting his life in order. His greatness has excited extreme views. At times even Swift himself appears to have had mixed feelings, and to have exercised discretion about revealing them.

Swift became many things in the Moor Park household: amanuensis, editor, confidential assistant and agent for Temple, and, on one occasion, messenger to King William III. He also became tutor to the younger daughter of a servant in the household, Esther Johnson, later called 'Stella' by Swift. Ultimately, Temple made Swift his literary executor, as well as her guardian. During Stella's lifetime there was speculation about her parentage; it was presumed that she was Sir William Temple's own child. Much later the possibility that she was the child of his younger sibling, Henry, was put forward.

We know a good deal about this period in Swift's life. We have, first of all, an important statement by him dealing with his arrival at Moor Park, the 'Ode to the Honble Sir William Temple'.[8] At the outset of Swift's time at Moor Park it seems that Temple was at his other house at Sheen, so that we find this young graduate, fresh from Ireland, sitting in the great man's home while the great man is away somewhere else, and penning an elaborate ode in the Cowley manner. Its main emphasis is on a prospective future life as a Poet, but it is crafted around the admiration Swift felt for the quality of virtue he recognized in Temple. Stanza by stanza the confessed inadequacies of the author of the Ode are contrasted with the real merits and achievements of the great man who is being addressed.

What is uniquely important about the Ode is the fact that it is almost certainly a contemporary account. It may never have been seen by Temple, though as a poet himself of modest achievement he would probably have been understanding and sympathetic. It is also the earliest surviving account of himself by Swift. Its 1689 date has been disputed; yet it is difficult to imagine Swift writing such a piece later on in their relationship.

The first stay in Moor Park was brief, lasting just over a year, and from it we have no other writing by Swift. He was sent by Temple back to Ireland in May 1690, carrying with him a letter from his patron to the King's Secretary of State, Robert Southwell. Southwell had served as a diplomat in Portugal and had corresponded with Temple. He was Irish, from a Kinsale landowning family, and had succeeded his father as vice-admiral of Munster in the year of Swift's birth. He was also a close friend of the Duke of Ormonde, and was related by marriage to Sir William Petty.

The event that took Swift back to Ireland was to be the culmination of a growing crisis: the Jacobite threat to the Glorious Revolution. King William III was engaged on a campaign the outcome of which would seriously affect the balance of power between Catholic and Protestant Europe. Sir William Temple, who had spent much of his diplomatic career engaged in the detailed pursuit of the Protestant and Restoration interests of England in Holland, and moreover was well informed about affairs in Ireland, was

King William III, by Godfrey Kneller, mezzotint by Andrew Miller, detail, left, *and Sir Robert Southwell, by Kneller, mezzotint by J. Smith*

supremely aware of the nature of the threat. South-well, also previously a diplomat, was well acquainted with Temple. Elrington Ball says that Southwell was 'considered by his contemporaries, especially by the great Duke of Ormonde, a man of singular discernment, prudence and ability'.[9] Ball also refers to Southwell's considerable knowledge of Ireland, which justified the King's choice of him as his Secretary of State. Southwell's commission was to accompany the King on the journey to Carrickfergus on the eve of a vital royal campaign. In the event, the evidence is insufficient to establish whether or not Swift took up the commission to work with Southwell in Ireland. Certainly, without the Temple–Southwell introduction

Swift would not have been able to make the crossing to Ireland in the midst of the Jacobite uprising, nor remain in the troubled country for several months. But he did make the crossing, and he did remain in the country, which reinforces the supposition that he took up the commission.

Swift himself, writing in the third person in his 'Autobiographical Fragment', advances an unlikely explanation for the journey to Ireland: his illness from eating a surfeit of fruit. 'Upon this Occasion he returned to Ireld, by advice of Physicians, who weakly imagined that his native air might be of some use to recover his Health. But growing worse, he soon went back to Sir Wm Temple; with whom growing into some confidence he was often trusted with matters of great Importance.'[10] This account obfuscates, perhaps deliberately, the extraordinary circumstances of his presence in a country where a serious war was being waged, and explains nothing of the time spent there.[11]

Swift's early years at Moor Park have been seen as apprentice years; the inference is that he climbed slowly to favour and importance in his patron's eyes. Temple's letter to Southwell, written just a year after Swift's arrival at Moor Park, would suggest otherwise. What Temple is doing, in that letter, is consigning his young protégé to the King's right-hand man at the outset of a great military campaign. The young man who is being offered by Temple 'has Latin and Greek, some French, writes a very good and current hand, is very honest and diligent, and has good friends, though they have for the present lost their fortunes, and his whole family having been long known to me oblige me thus far to take care of him'.[12] There is nothing restrained or doubting in Temple's endorsement. Temple is not necessarily furthering Swift's career only for Swift's sake; it is tempting to speculate that Temple wanted to receive from Swift first-hand intelligence on the country in which he grew up and in which he still held property, and where other members of his family, including his brother, had even more extensive interests.

While in Ireland, Swift began his 'Ode to the King on His Irish Expedition and the Success of His Arms in general'. Whether he finished it there, or later, at Moor Park, is not known, but the intense and passionate tone in which it is composed would suggest rapid composition, a view reinforced by the fact that his next work was 'rough drawn in a week, and finished in two days after'.[13] He was getting the hang of things, even if the pindaric form was shortly to be dropped in favour of couplets.[14]

We have no clear dates for Swift's return from Ireland. He visited his mother in Leicester, and stayed with her long enough to engage in flirtation with a local girl, possibly more than one. It seems he also travelled by way of Oxford where he stayed for a short time, probably for the purpose of visiting his cousin Thomas Swift. Then he went on to Moor Park. He was to return to Oxford the following summer, when he obtained his master's degree. He was soon to engage directly in writing his 'Ode to the Athenian Society', whose work was of some interest to Temple,

and indeed to Swift. This Ode was also Swift's first
appearance in print. He sent it with a letter dated 14
February 1692 from Moor Park, and both were published in *The Athenian Gazette* that March. In the
accompanying letter Swift refers to being in Ireland
the previous year, 'from whence I returned about half
a year ago', a half year during which time he read all
the publications of the Society.

Both the poem and the letter express the writer's
admiration for the far-ranging inquiry that went on
within the Society.[15] The Ode is cast in enthusiastic
terms, uses war metaphors which link it to the 'Ode to
the King', and is momentarily quite witty. In a mar-
ginal note Swift refers directly to the preceding composition, 'the Ode I writ to the King in Ireland'. The
new poem is certainly more assured than the earlier
Odes, and looks forward to the remaining poems in
the early canon of Swift's work—'Ode to Dr William
Sancroft', 'To Mr Congreve', and '[Lines] Occasioned
by Sir W— T—'s Late Illness and Recovery'.

On the evidence of his work, of his few letters dating from this time, and of Temple's testimonial letter
to Southwell, it is hard not to form the opinion that
he viewed Moor Park as his home, that he came and
went freely. He enjoyed the confidence and support
of his patron, and spent a great deal of time writing:
'I have writ, and burnt and writ again, upon almost all
manner of subjects, more perhaps than any man in
England', he wrote to the Reverend John Kendall.[16]

While it is clear that the pindaric form in poetry is
ill-suited to Swift's mature voice, it did correspond

with his youthful energy and his essentially passionate nature. He was precisely what Temple wanted at this time, a writer both gifted and spirited to help him during his closing years and to put his papers in order, with a view to further publication. Swift reinforced his capabilities, in Temple's eyes, with a manner and form in his writing that was respectful to the point of being adulatory. Among Temple's dearly loved children, all of whom at this stage had pre-deceased him, there was nothing comparable to the talent Swift displayed from his arrival at Moor Park. And whatever other reasons there may have been for the sustained association between the two men, Swift's ability to write was a powerful cement in their developing relationship. Allowing for the forty years between them in age, their mutual dependence and their common love for language, debate and writing created what amounted to a real friendship.

At the request of the Bishop of Ely, Swift began an 'Ode to Dr William Sancroft, Late Lord Archbishop of Canterbury' in May 1692, but he failed to finish it. Two further poems followed in 1693, one of them an attempt to renew contact with his friend of school and university days, William Congreve, whose successful early plays *The Old Batchelor* and *The Double-Dealer* inspired Swift. They made him envious as well, and the poem conveys complicated emotional contradictions. Congreve had behind him the powerful hand of Dryden, who helped to achieve the performance of his first play and saw in Congreve his heir in the field of drama. Swift envisaged that the lines might appear

*William Congreve, by Godfrey
Kneller, mezzotint by J. Smith*

as a 'Prologue' for the printed version of *The Double-
Dealer*, but before offering them he wrote to his
cousin Thomas Swift (who had advised him to keep
the poem to himself): 'I desire you will send me word
immediately how it [the play] succeeded, whether
well, ill or indifferently, because my sending them to
Mr Congreve depends upon knowing the issue.'[17]
Swift thought the verses would serve for any of his
former schoolfriend's plays.

   He wrote also at this time a second poem addressed
to his patron. The dutiful '[Lines] Occasioned by Sir
W— T—'s Late Illness and Recovery' tells us little
about the illness, and surprisingly little about Temple

generally. But it is a confident expression of Swift's poetic skill, of which this is the last surviving example until the mature voice emerges at the end of the decade, mainly in octosyllabic couplets.

That he had the full confidence of Temple is demonstrated by his being sent to the Palace of Kensington to present to the King, and at much greater length to the King's favourite, the Earl of Portland, Temple's views on the Triennial Bill. This was a re-enactment of Charles I's Triennial Act, requiring a new House of Commons every three years. Swift delivered a document from Temple on which he gave a verbal gloss, speaking briefly to the King, and at length to Portland. Nearly four decades later Swift wrote sourly of this encounter with the Court: 'This was the first time that Mr Swift had ever any converse with courts, and he told his friends it was the first incident that helped to cure him of vanity.'[18] But his vanity at the time was of a different order; and William Temple's sister, Lady Martha Giffard, in a letter to her niece, Lady Berkeley, wrote: 'I have sent him with another compliment from Papa to the King, where I fancy he is not displeased with finding occasions of going.'[19]

Swift expected his career to be helped forward as a result of his services to Temple. He made his inclination to enter the Church, which he had formulated during his time at Moor Park, contingent on getting a preferment. It did not happen. Some kind of breach occurred between the two men in 1694, occasioned by Swift's departure from Moor Park, Temple, understandably, not wishing him to go. Swift told his cousin Deane that Temple 'was extremely angry I left him'; apparently his patron was reluctant to give Swift any clear assurances about what his employment or role in the household might be.[20] The implication is that this related in some way to Temple's papers, which clearly justified collecting and editing. In the absence of Swift, Temple employed as secretary Swift's cousin, Thomas, whose shortcomings seem to have been a factor in the return of Swift and his reconciliation with Temple. In the period of disaffection Swift wrote a very humble letter seeking urgent endorsement from Temple in the form of a 'certificate of my behaviour' while at Moor Park.[21] Temple readily endorsed his protégé for holy orders, and in due course the friendship between the two men was fully restored.

This episode is one of several which strengthen the view of Swift as a permanent resident at Moor Park and not just a secretary, arriving, serving for a time, and departing.[22] His career as it developed, and his private ambitions, were no impediment to his continuing presence in the household.

He was ordained in Christ Church Cathedral, and at the instigation of an unknown person was given the parish of Kilroot, east of Carrickfergus. He hated it, stayed for a year, then returned to Moor Park. During his stay in Ireland he may have sketched out in greater detail *A Tale of a Tub*, his first important work, and one of his most enjoyable. His experiences in the countryside around Carrickfergus, an area dominated by Dissenters, is always credited with inspiring the work. Dating it is difficult. Traditionally, he created the original allegory while at Trinity College, and John Lyon, a prebendary of St Patrick's and manager of Swift's affairs in his later years, claims that people may have seen it there or in his parish at Kilroot. Perhaps it was shelved during the early years at Moor Park, on account of Temple's lack of sympathy for the art of satire, and then, after Swift had been enriched by the period in Ireland, the *Tale* reached fruition during the last spell at Moor Park, though it was not to be published until 1704.[23]

The Kilroot sojourn did produce Swift's only known proposal of marriage, to Jane Waring, whom he called 'Varina'. Despite their high-flown rhetoric, his letters to her ring false, and there is something artificial in the conjunction of an offer of marriage with the information that he is being encouraged to return to Moor Park and take up once again his duties there.

In short, Madam, I am once more offered the advantage to have the same acquaintance with greatness that I formerly enjoyed, and with better prospect of interest. I here solemnly offer to forgo it all for your sake. I desire nothing of your fortune; you shall live where and with whom you please till my affairs are settled to your desire, and in the meantime I will push my advancement with all the eagerness and courage imaginable, and do not doubt to succeed.[24]

It is a long letter; and, oddly, it has all the appearances of being for public, or posterity's, consumption. It concludes: 'Farewell, Madam, and my love make you awhile forget your temper to do me justice. Only remember, that if you still refuse to be mine, you will quickly lose, for ever lose, him that is resolved to die as he has lived, all yours. Jon. Swift.' She did refuse to become his wife, or to make any promise in that direction. And there the matter rested for some time.

The second literary work of importance belonging to this early period, in which Swift was finding the true expression of his nature in satire, was *The Battle of the Books*, a mock-treatise on the conflict between the Ancients and the Moderns. If *A Tale of a Tub* had greater contemporary impact, and was in absolute terms a more substantial work, *The Battle of the Books* is Swift's humorous, satirical contribution to an endless human argument between the intellectual benefits and authority of the past and those of the present. Its immediate inspiration was not so much what Sir William Temple had said in his essay 'Of Ancient and Modern Learning' (1690), but the fact that Temple made a passing reference to *The Epistles of Phalaris*, which were subsequently shown to be fraudulent. The exposure fuelled an energetic controversy. *The Battle of the Books* was Swift's comment on it.

The so-called 'Battle', between the authority of ancient learning and the challenge of modern thought, has been present in one form or another in every century. Great seventeenth-century minds— Descartes, Bacon, Galileo, Newton, and others—had brought the discussion to a head. The argument was conducted in every field of human inspiration and performance. Aeschylus holds his place against

Racine; Plato and Aristotle are read and have a following for the eternal value of their thought. Temple's invasion of this inexhaustible debating territory was modest, mannerly, well judged and philosophically correct. What he attacks is pedantry. His references to the *Epistles* are insignificant, and he was essentially right in claiming that excellence in thought or in artistic creation was a product of no system, but of the individual's judgment and integrity.

There is no real argument, at least not with the benefit of hindsight. Swift's own view is that advance in human thought, in creative work, is as inescapable as are the lasting achievements of the past. No authority can rest exclusively with the Ancients, nor with the Moderns. Swift's only option, as a young witness to a grave debate, was to make a joke of it for posterity, rescuing his patron from his minor error regarding the *Epistles*, and punishing the 'schoolmen' for the uncompromising virulence of their assault. In this way he offers his own resolution to the conflict, though it was not published until 1704, well after the immediate row had died down.

Sir William Temple died in January 1699 when Swift was thirty-three and in the prime of his life. Their ten-year friendship had transformed that life; living and working with the retired statesman had given Swift self-confidence, a position in the world, and the guidance and example of a remarkable career. Temple's decision to make Swift his literary executor meant that the younger man would redeploy the exemplary life in the publication of the Works. As

[45]

Walter Scott says, since 'all Swift's plans revolve upon making himself eminent as an author, the value of such an occasion to distinguish himself could scarcely be too highly estimated'.[25] Though Swift wished otherwise, this, in the end, was the route, and the only route, to the success he was to have in life. He was not rewarded or taken care of in terms of Church appointment, or even prospects in that direction. He was never to enjoy such privileges, and the rewards he had were always less than he felt he merited. But in the household of Sir William Temple during the 1690s he learned a trade, found his voice as a writer, and defined many of the attitudes which were to govern his future life.

III

Between Ireland and England

Shortly after Temple's death, Swift was invited by the Earl of Berkeley, one of the Lords Justices of Ireland, to go there as his chaplain and secretary. It is possible that the invitation derived indirectly from his dead patron, but this is unclear. Swift sailed with the Earl's party from Bristol to Waterford in August 1699. With remarkable rapidity, Swift was superseded in the position of secretary by an older man, Arthur Bushe, who was a friend of Henry Ryder, Swift's teacher in Kilkenny. Bushe met the Earl's party on the outskirts of Dublin and travelled the final miles in the Earl's coach, apparently ingratiating himself. The usurpation rankled for years.

Swift also anticipated that he might succeed Coote

Ormsby as Dean of Derry in January 1700. But again he was 'cheated' of this, or so his own account would have us believe. In fact, he simply did not have the necessary experience or standing in the Church. As Ehrenpreis has written, it was 'a lifelong trait of Swift's that he enjoyed reviving, exaggerating, and contemplating the injustices which he thought he had suffered'.[26] Inexperienced, lacking skill or cunning in gaining preferment, he was on his own, and confronted with the job of making his way. The wise and powerful patronage of Sir William Temple, which had lasted through ten years, was a thing of the past.

He did not come away empty-handed from these bruising experiences. Dr John Bolton, who became Dean of Derry, vacated important ecclesiastical livings which passed to Swift. One was Laracor, in County Meath, the very name of which evokes a strand of contentment and fulfilment in Swift's existence. It yielded income. It gave him land, on which he was to lavish attention. And with it went a stall in the Cathedral of St Patrick in Dublin. He also retained the domestic chaplaincy to the Earl of Berkeley, which gave him two advantages: ready access to the society of Dublin Castle, and a friendship with the earl's daughter, Lady Betty Berkeley, which was to last for a number of years.

He wrote at this time a set of 'rules' on a single page, with the heading 'When I come to be old 1699', and the admonishment at the end 'Not to sett up for observing all these Rules; for fear I should observe none.' They are mainly about restraints and reservations: 'Not to marry a young Woman ... keep young Company ... be fond of Children ... be covetous ... talk much, nor of my self ... be positive ... boast of my former beauty.'[27] They are the strictures of an alert and cautious disposition. Turned inward on himself they suggest a rational acceptance of limitations and represent one side of Swift's character at a point which is essentially a watershed in his affairs.

In 1700 Jane Waring re-opened with Swift the possibility of marriage. It was a mistake on her part, a misjudgment of the present situation and of the past. She clearly had no sense of what had changed in four years. Swift confronted the unwelcome overture, made through his uncle Adam, in a cold and unfeeling letter that amounted to a rejection, by putting in her way conditions of compliance which must have seemed at best unloving, at worst arrogant and intolerant. It has the effect of making one feel for her, despite knowing so little of her personality and character. One traces in the words the shiver of dismissal and rejection which must have run through her body as her mind assessed the bewildering force of his cold reasoning:

I desire, therefore, you will let me know if your health be otherwise than it was when you told me the doctors advised you against marriage, as what would certainly hazard your life. Are they or you grown of another opinion in this particular? Are you in a condition to manage domestic affairs, with an income of less perhaps than three hundred pounds a year? Have you such an inclination to my person and humour, as

to comply with my desires and way of living, and endeavour
to make us both as happy as you can? Will you be ready to
engage in those methods I shall direct for the improvement
of your mind, so as to make us entertaining company for each
other, without being miserable when we are neither visiting
nor visited? Can you bend your love and esteem and indifference to others the same way as I do mine? Shall I have so much
power in your heart, or you so much government of your passions, as to grow in good humour upon my approach ...? Have
you so much good-nature as to endeavour by soft words to
smooth any rugged humour occasioned by the cross acci-
dents of life? ... These are the questions I have always
resolved to propose to her with whom I meant to pass my
life; and whenever you can heartily answer them in the affir-
mative, I shall be blessed to have you in my arms, without
regarding whether your person be beautiful, or your fortune
large. Cleanliness in the first, and competency in the other, is
all I look for. I desire, indeed, a plentiful revenue, but would
rather it should be of my own; though I should bear from a
wife to be reproached for the greatest.[28]

In 1701 he published his first short book, *A Dis-
course of the Contests and Dissensions between the Nobles
and the Commons in Athens and Rome*. Less dry than it
sounds, it was a political pamphlet, contemporary in
its theme. Another London undertaking was his work
on William Temple's papers. Under the provocation
of a spurious edition of Temple's letters, Swift com-
menced his work as literary executor, publishing a
first volume of Temple's works in 1701. At this time,
though at no other, Swift travelled regularly between
Ireland and England, carrying out his work as editor
in London and fulfilling his Church duties in Ireland.[28]

Most significantly of all, he arranged that Esther Johnson, his former pupil at Moor Park, together with her lifelong companion, Rebecca Dingley, should move to Dublin. Stella had land in Ireland, left to her by Temple. Elaborate additional reasons for the move have been suggested. The probable truth is that she constituted for Swift his only 'family' and had no future prospects in England for the kind of guardian-ship which Swift promised, and which he certainly delivered for the rest of her life. Her last recorded visit to England was in 1708.

Swift's writing began to attract attention. In the small, tightly controlled and monarchical political system of the time, political and artistic power went hand in hand. Certain writers were 'preferred'; Prior and Congreve had political benefits showered on them, and there is no doubt that Swift sought the same, with less success. He was noticed by members of the Whig Junto then in power, including Charles Spencer, Earl of Sunderland, and Charles Montagu, Earl of Halifax, who had been at school with Prior and was his patron.

Swift was known as a Whig at this time, with some justification, though more needs to be said about his politics. To be seen as a Whig was a matter of politi-cal calculation more than inner conviction. Moreover, Sir William Temple had been a Whig, and Swift numbered among his friends many who were of the Whig persuasion. But at heart he was not in favour of the occasional conformity favoured by the Whigs in the interest of Dissenters operating in public life, and he mistrusted as a result Whig good faith towards the Established Church. However, the Whigs were regularly in power during these years of parliamentary instability, and as a writer and man of wit, as well as someone who needed to remain in close touch with writers and politicians, he kept to himself his deeper convictions about serious political issues.

Swift's politics need also to be seen in the context of historical events. When William III died in 1702 and was succeeded by James II's Protestant daughter, Anne, an important shift occurred in public interest and political focus. The primary interests of the Whig administration centred on the European war, which was being prosecuted by the Duke of Marlborough and his son-in-law, the Earl of Godolphin. The war, in which Britain was allied with the Dutch and the Austrians, had as its principal objective the prevention of an alliance between France and Spain. The important trading corollary was to keep open the seas for New and Old World profit. All of William III's instincts were in support of protecting a balance of power which favoured British and Dutch interests. Queen Anne had different priorities. She was a devout Protestant, her piety was renowned, and her determination to protect the Church was both fervent and practical. Swift was shrewd enough to see the significance of the Queen casting her eye favourably on the Tories— though it would be eight years before they formed an administration. It was a sympathy that derived in part from her Stuart origins, in part from having far less enthusiasm for commerce and international trade

Queen Anne, by Godfrey Kneller, engraved by J. Houbraken

than her Dutch predecessor. As early as 1704 Swift's inner instincts and beliefs were directing him towards a change in his political stance.

Swift was uncertain about how to advance his own interests, and he was slow to move away from his Whig friends; consequently, he was reluctant about displaying his High Church convictions. He was handicapped, when he came on visits to England, by the fact that he was coming from Ireland. He was effectively an outsider, not directly patronized by any great political figure. He had friends (we would call them 'contacts' today); but reliance on them for help in advancing his position seems to have been extremely difficult for Swift. He had limited financial resources, and could not sustain a life in London without the preferment which it was his increasingly forlorn purpose to obtain. Moreover, he had Church duties to perform. The Archbishop of Dublin, William King, was a demanding diocesan cleric; and his rules were greatly reinforced by the fact that Swift loved his life at Laracor and was enchanted to have, as his Irish 'family', Esther Johnson and Rebecca Dingley.

He published *A Tale of a Tub* in May 1704. Unwisely, he dedicated it to John Somers, the former Lord Chancellor who had exercised great power during the reign of William III. Somers was a great lawyer, and a gifted and loyal friend to many writers, but he was a Whig, and out of favour with the Queen, and the dedication reinforced the conviction of readers that Swift was attacking the Church. The satire

John, Lord Somers, by Richardson,
mezzotint by J. Smith

was controversial in the new, strait-laced circumstances of Queen Anne's reign, yet seemed well suited to the problem of reconciling the conflicting interests of an established Church and a solid nonconformist minority. It was published with *The Battle of the Books*. Further satires followed, none of which bore Swift's name as author.

With no serious prospect of advancement in England, and a life in Ireland which gave him much pleasure and contentment, Swift spent the four years following the publication of *A Tale of a Tub* attending to his parish duties and enjoying the company of Stella and Rebecca Dingley. In 1707 Thomas Herbert,

Thomas Herbert, eighth Earl of Pembroke, by William Wissing, mezzotint by J. Smith, and Sir Andrew Fountaine, by Armstrong, engraving by W.C. Edwards

eighth Earl of Pembroke, became Lord Lieutenant with the specific purpose of having the Sacramental Test abolished in Ireland. Swift opposed this. So did a substantial majority in Parliament. Since this nullified the political objectives of the Lord Lieutenant, Pembroke was able to devote his time to wit, drollery, punning and other diversions, which he pursued in the company of Swift, whom he befriended from the start of his short tenure in office. He was amused in particular by Swift's ability at making puns.[30]

Pembroke, a distinguished statesman to whom the period of service in Ireland was little short of banishment, brought with him Sir Andrew Fountaine and made him Usher of the Black Rod in the Dublin Parliament. Fountaine became an even closer friend of Swift's and a devoted admirer of his talents. He also later became part of the Van Homrigh circle in London. He was a man of property and wealth. He was a virtuoso, one of those 'who dwell in a higher region than other mortals', and his house in Norfolk contained a fine collection of Grand Tour sculptures, paintings and other rarities.

At this time the Church of Ireland faced the overriding problem of the First Fruits and Twentieth Parts. These fees paid by clergymen to the Crown had been remitted by Queen Anne in England in 1701. The Church of Ireland wanted the same favour, known as 'Queen Anne's Bounty'. With small parishes and churches which had fallen into disrepair, this penal tax, or tithe, was an insupportable burden. Swift's connections in London were recognized. He was seen as an ideal plenipotentiary to those in power, and duly came under instruction from Archbishop King and the Primate to petition the Whig administration for the Queen's remittance of the tax. Charged with this task, he returned to England, in the company, as it happened, of Pembroke, whose mission in Ireland over the Sacramental Test was over, and who was himself heading to higher office as Lord High Admiral, a post he had previously held in 1702.

It was a great moment in Swift's life. He once more had a commission that required his negotiating skills and his contacts, and that justified his calling as a churchman interested in political issues. He was going from a poor country to one which was increasingly prosperous, and he noticed and commented on the difference. Moreover, he had persuaded Stella and Dingley to pay what was to be their last visit to England, and to stay in London or outside it for a period of some months. He was in high spirits at the prospect of once more engaging in the social life of London, which brought together the poets, wits, playwrights, essayists, philosophers and politicians, many of them titled, in a close and lively social whirl.

This was the age of the coffee house, the pamphlet, the weekly papers such as *The Tatler*, Court receptions, overt patronage and flamboyant entertaining, and Swift had several passports to entitle him to entry. He renewed contact with the Earl of Berkeley and his daughter, Lady Betty Berkeley. He had entertained her and her mother, the Countess, on his previous visit, teasing them into believing that his brilliant little trifle, *Meditation on a Broomstick*, had been written by the tedious Robert Boyle, from whose *Meditations* Swift read aloud to her on a visit to Berkeley Castle. He inserted his manuscript into the pages, passing it off as a serious expression of wisdom, to everyone's eventual delight, and to the banishment of Boyle's book.

On that same visit, after crossing St George's Channel with the Earl of Pembroke, Swift had travelled to Leicester, and called on his mother there, spending some days with her before continuing on his way to London. He stopped at an inn in Dunstable,

Bedfordshire, and there occurred an encounter which was to change the course of his life.

A

T A L E
OF A
T U B.

Written for the Univerſal Improvement of Mankind.

Diu multumque deſideratum

To which is added,

An A C C O U N T of a
B A T T E L
BETWEEN THE
Antient and Modern B O O K S
in St. *James*'s Library.

Baſima eacabaſa eanaa irrauriſta, diarba da caeotaba fobor camelanthi. *Iren. Lib* 1 C. 18.

——— *Juvatque novos decerpere flores,*
Inſignemque meo capiti petere inde coronam,
Unde prius nulli velarunt tempora Muſæ Lucret.

L O N D O N.
Printed for *John Nutt*, near *Stationers-Hall.*
MDCCIV.

Esther Van Homrigh, doubtful portrait by Philip Hussey

IV

Spilled Coffee and First Fruits

Swift's meeting with Esther Van Homrigh, in 1707, changed the direction of both their lives. It was recorded, with erotic overtones, in later correspondence. It was the start of their love affair. Yet it was clearly not the first encounter, either between Swift and the woman he called Vanessa, or between him and other members of her family. Vanessa's father, Bartholomew Van Homrigh, who had died four years before, had been a fairly prominent figure in Dublin life, almost certainly known to Swift, through civic, Castle and Church circles. He had served William III during the campaigns against the Jacobites, provisioning the army in Ireland, and there is a distinct possibility that he was in the King's party, along with

Southwell and Swift, when they landed at Carrickfergus in the 1690 campaign. He was a member of the Dublin Philosophical Society. Van Homrigh's wife, giddy, gossipy, socially confident and ambitious, the daughter of a Commissioner of Revenue, would have fitted well into the Court life surrounding both the Earl of Berkeley, when he was in Dublin as a Lord Justice, and the Earl of Pembroke, during his short stay at Lord Lieutenant.

But if Swift met Vanessa in the company of one or both of her parents—in her own right she was a Freewoman of the City of Dublin—the meeting was different in kind from the encounter in Dunstable in 1707, when she spilled coffee and in some captivating way ensnared his affections.

The meeting took place in December. Swift was then just forty. Vanessa, in her twentieth year, was in Dunstable with her mother and the rest of the family en route from Dublin to London. The encounter was important enough to be recalled by Swift, in an affectionate letter to her many years later, as the comencement of their love for each other; it was a prologue, and it was to be followed by 'two hundred chapters of madness'. He listed some of these; he hinted at many others. Swift's letters entice Vanessa in the manner of a lover, with 'Do you remember …? Have you forgotten …?' He wrote such words to no other woman. He left no indication, in poem, letter, notebook or account book, of a parallel set of feelings. In the compass of his whole life, which was one of vicissitudes and disappointments, the glowing, vital, turbulent love affair with this much younger woman, whose intellect he so admired, is a singular episode.[31]

He was confused about it. He turned this way and that in his efforts to deny himself. But the contrast between the stilted language of his letters to Varina, and the vivid accounts he gives of his own and Vanessa's doings in *their* correspondence, is compelling. One's heart goes out to Swift in his delusion. Did he really believe that this was *not* love? Did he pretend to be in decline, when he was busy conquering the world? Could he with justice claim that his thoughts had been wholly directed at the formation and cultivation of her mind? Was he really a falling oak, a ship decayed? Was he a vessel in which a young girl could not entrust her future? What remote consistency is there between such a view and the loving words of a man to a young girl, as he tells her his remembrance of the most agreeable chamber in the whole world, the one in which the two of them, close together and alone, take coffee, or with their lips and mouths savour the tart tang of a home-grown orange, dipped for sweetness in a bowl of sugar, then crushed and sucked and swallowed down?

He referred to the event in Dunstable as 'the time of spilling the Coffee'. The linking of this with love is clear enough. It is contained in a letter written in August 1720, a long and affectionate reply to one in which Vanessa had openly referred to 'being in love'. Swift asks her, 'What would you give to have the History of Cad— and [Vanessa] exactly written through all its steps from the beginning to this time. I believe

it would do well in Verse, and be as long as the other.
I hope it will be done. It ought to be an exact Chronicle of 12 years, from the time of spilling the Coffee
to drinking of Coffee, from Dunstable to Dublin,
with every single passage since.'[32]

It was an extraordinary suggestion. *Cadenus and
Vanessa*, which told the story of how Swift and
Vanessa had fallen in love, was the longest poem, by
far, of Swift's career as a writer, epic in proportion.[33]
And here he was offering the same again. It is just one
of the many indications of how Swift viewed those
'chapters of madness', and how he now viewed
Vanessa, twelve years later. Their relationship, 'from
the time of spilling the Coffee', when it had quickly
become affectionate and intimate, to the beginning of
the 1720s, when his love for her was still evident in
his writing, was that of lovers. It was more, besides: he
helped her with her financial and legal affairs; was
involved with other members of her family; shared in
her social life. But within that 'exact Chronicle',
which was probably never set down, there existed for
Swift a unique set of feelings which posterity has con-
sistently sought to belittle, to dismiss, to deny, or to
explain to the detriment of Vanessa's character.

Vanessa was swept up in the vigorous, enthusiastic
and essentially optimistic affairs of this dynamic cler-
gyman from the city of her own birth. Swift was to
remain in London for eighteen months, between the
winter of 1707 and the summer of 1709, carefully
recording his daily affairs, keeping minutely detailed
accounts of sums lost playing cards with named

friends, including Vanessa and her circle, or cash paid to servants in the houses he visited.[34]

The actual spilling of the coffee at Dunstable, in December 1707, was clearly an innocent enough event. But it came to be used by Swift and Vanessa as part of their own private language, indicating a great deal more than consumption of a beverage. He reminds her on one occasion 'that riches are nine parts in ten of all that is good in life, and health is the tenth. Drinking Coffee comes long after, and yet it is the eleventh; but without the two former you cannot drink it right.' In that same letter he refers to a rendezvous which they seem to have used, 'where one might pass three or four hours in drinking coffee in the morning, or dining tête-à-tête, and drinking coffee again till seven'.[35] There are many other such references. The general sense is of intimacy between lovers, being alone together and enjoying the privacy of this.

Sir Andrew Fountaine had a town house in Leicester Fields, now Leicester Square, and offered to accommodate Swift when they all reached London. Both Fountaine and the Earl of Pembroke were important to Swift in his primary purpose at that time, which was to obtain remission for the Church of Ireland of the First Fruits and Twentieth Parts. Travelling as a plenipotentiary for the Church he wrote to the Archbishop of Dublin, William King, from his mother's house, on 6 December, that the association with Pembroke was a stepping-stone to other great men who might help in the project, in particular Lord

Leicester Fields, London, by T. Bowles, engraved by B.F. Leizel

Somers and the Earl of Sunderland. Fountaine was the link between Swift and Pembroke, and his offer of accommodation was clearly seized on by Swift for reasons beyond mere convenience.

Fountaine's house was but a short walk from Charles Street, now Charles II Street, which was where the Van Homrigh family took rooms, at The Two Green Flower Pots, run by Mr Goodere. From the moment they were all settled in London, Swift became a regular caller. It seems he paid several early visits during December and January, and it was at this time that, through the Van Homrighs, he met Miss Anne Long, a well-known London beauty and a 'toast' of the Kit-Cat Club.[36] Her father, Sir James Long, had an estate in Wiltshire, where, it was said, he looked down on the Earls of Pembroke, his neighbours at Wilton, because they had come late to the country, and from *Wales*. She was also a cousin of the Van Homrighs, and she lived nearby, in Albemarle Street, where at some stage she had living with her Isaac Newton's niece Catherine Barton, also a beauty, whose relationship with Lord Halifax is supposed to have given cause for scandal.

Swift drew up a humourous 'Treaty of Acquaintance' with Miss Long, which sheds light on his attitude to diversion and entertainment, and on the social atmosphere in the Van Homrigh household. Although the *Decree for Concluding the Treaty between Dr Swift and Mrs Long* was later dated 1709, and so appears in various editions, it belongs to the first days of Swift's arrival in London in 1708.[37] It contains in the preamble a reference to 'Dr Swift, of Leicester Fields'. Archbishop King continued to use the address, and as late as March he was sending letters to Swift 'Care of Sir Andrew Fountaine, Leicester Fields'.

Anne Long, as a 'toast', enjoyed the privilege of being free to choose the men paying attentions to her. It was this that brought about Swift's document, since he was not of a mind to play the kinds of deferential games associated with members of the Kit-Cat Club.

The terms of the *Decree* express it precisely. Swift, 'upon the score of his Merit, and extraordinary Qualities, doth claim the sole and undoubted Right, That all Persons whatsoever, shall make such Advances to him, as he pleases to demand'. In the Decree, Mrs Van Homrigh and her daughter were strictly forbidden 'to aid, abett, comfort or encourage the said Mrs *Long*, in her Disobedience for the Future'. The *Decree*, which was issued 'By Especial Command', was signed by the youngest Van Homrigh, Vanessa's younger brother Ginkel. This sparkling and ingenious *jeu d'esprit* was, then, a family affair, involving Mrs Van Homrigh, her daughter, her son Ginkel and of course her cousin.

The relationship between Swift and Vanessa clearly embraced some of the happiest and most successful years in Swift's life. For joy and fulfilment, unshadowed by setback or difficulty, it is hard to find an alternative *annus mirabilis* to 1708. Deane Swift writes of it thus: 'We may observe the genius of DR. SWIFT to break forth upon us in the year 1708 with such an astonishing blaze of humour, politicks, religion, patriotism, wit and poetry; that if the world had been totally unacquainted with all his former reputation, the productions of that one year would have been highly sufficient to have established his fame unto all eternity.'[38]

He followed the private jest of the *Decree* with several others of a more public nature, and it is difficult not to associate Vanessa, her mother, the brothers, sister Moll, and Anne Long herself, with Swift's other

activities at the time. He does not record such partic-
ipation; his lists, assembled years later in letters to
Vanessa, are all of private matters, intimate, secret
and emotional. But the creative background remained
his writing, and publicly it was of a kind to invite
laughter, wonder, shock, and great admiration. His
pamphlets and poems became the talk of London,
and circulated in other cities of the realm and on the
Continent. And they almost certainly provided an
additional frisson of entertainment and talk among
those closest to him. Everything points to the Van
Homrigh circle as providing the *dramatis personae* for
his immediate entertainment, and not unreasonably
looking for entertainment from him into the bargain.
The circle, now and later, included Lady Betty Butler
(daughter of the Duke of Ormonde), Lady Betty
Berkeley, Sir Andrew Fountaine, Mrs Armstrong and
her sister Lady Catherine Lucy, Charles Ford, Henry
St John, Erasmus Lewis, Joseph Addison, and a number of others. Some of the activities in which he
plunged himself were sensational, like the assault on
the reputation of the popular astrologer John Partridge, which saw the creation of the character of
'Isaac Bickerstaff'.[39] It is not unreasonable to imagine
the small groups with whom he played picquet or
ombre, and visited during the evenings, as constitut-
ing an audience for his wit and his writing.

The Partridge jest, which lasted no more than a
month or two, became the talk of salon, coffee house,
club and tavern. And of course Grub Street provided
the material, in a rapid succession of versions of each

and every publication, in varied format, with or without printer's name, place and date, in versions printed in Dublin, Edinburgh, and on the Continent, and in languages which included French, Dutch and German. What Swift had originally sold for a penny, the pirates sold for a halfpenny, and Partridge-shooting became the world's sport. Swift, meanwhile, learned that the cradle of the city's affairs lay in the hands of Grub Street, and that the sound sense of journals and journalists, of printers and street-sellers of ballads and other writings, prevailed as a national weather-vane.

Swift's correspondence at this time is mainly with William King, Archbishop of Dublin and the leading political figure in Church affairs in Ireland. The letters present a totally different side of Swift, conscientiously pursuing the matter of the First Fruits and Twentieth Parts. There is a fundamental difference between the Swift of 1704 and *A Tale of a Tub*, and the Swift engaged on Church business with politicians in 1708. He has changed irreversibly in his stature, assuming powers that he did not have before; and as a consequence of this he is resolving and rationalizing his own political, social, moral and religious views. In respect of the First Fruits themselves, his mission was unsuccessful. His immediate fate, in the spring of 1709, was one of a slightly ignominious return to parish duties in Ireland. Before leaving, however, he had encounters with the Earl of Wharton, who had been appointed Lord Lieutenant to succeed the Earl of Pembroke. Joseph Addison was Wharton's chief secretary. Swift made overtures to Wharton, and had a couple of

Thomas, first Earl of Wharton, by Godfrey Kneller, engraved by Cooper, and Joseph Addison, by Kneller, mezzotint by John Simon

unsatisfactory meetings, at which the Earl fobbed him off with excuses that he was not adequately informed and therefore not prepared to deal with the matter. Swift took exception to the Earl's treatment of him on their first encounter, and his antipathy grew subsequently. But he certainly did not have the same feelings towards Addison, who assured Swift of an appointment as chaplain to the Lord Lieutenant.

The appointment was incidental to the relationship between the two men. Swift recognized the value and the promise to himself which resided in the other writer. Addison was yet another example of the suc-

Richard Steele, by Thornhill, engraved by Vertue

cess displayed by his colleagues—if not rivals—who had effectively combined literature with politics, getting preferments of one kind or another from those in power. In Addison's case, this milking of the system was to go on for a further ten years; and, in a subtle way which cannot entirely have pleased Swift, Addison patronized him.

The relationship altered in Swift's favour later, when he returned to London. But at this time, with Addison the Lord Lieutenant's chief secretary, Swift found himself in the embarrassing position of needing to ingratiate himself. Theirs was a friendship which both worked and lasted, transcending the political differences between them, Addison remaining a confirmed Whig when Swift sided with the Tories. Its lasting memorial is in the pages of *The Tatler*, a publication which involved Richard Steele as well, though Steele's relationship with Swift was never as harmonious. Swift contributed to *The Tatler* under the name of Isaac Bickerstaff, or in unsigned pieces, but left London shortly after publication of number 32, and was back in Dublin for the following nine months. He later furnished material for the paper from Dublin. Swift, in these short essays, multiplied the layers of his satire, and retreated behind the walls of words which conceal his mixed and myriad purposes.

There is an abiding objective in these pieces: he wants to mock excesses in everything, including an excessive intellectuality detected at this time in his beloved Vanessa, a fault induced primarily by himself. This is a central theme in *Cadenus and Vanessa*, and also in his letters to her. He wants, in much of his writing, to hint at the frivolity of women, and its dangers, and at the seriousness of women, and *its* dangers. He wants to advise men to respect the minds as well as the hearts and bodies of those they love. His motive is love in the broadest sense, love of humanity, love of life. His self-protection is formed out of an innate and well-managed secretiveness, and this becomes a lifelong adventure story in which the best clues remain locked within his own heart and mind.

Esther Johnson, engraving after a drawing by Thomas Parnell;
this is the most nearly authentic portrait of Stella in existence

V

'Journal to Stella'

We do not know when Swift first used the name 'Stella' as a substitute for Esther Johnson's Christian name. It appears, as though it were already a familiar form of address, in the second letter of the *Journal to Stella*, 9 September 1710, and in subsequent letters in that collection. But it did not provide Swift with the title. Although he intended the collection of letters to Esther Johnson and Rebecca Dingley to hold together as a single 'work'—he calls his correspondence a 'journal'—the title was provided by Thomas Sheridan in his 1784 edition of Swift's *Works*. [40]

The *Journal to Stella* is a concentrated correspondence, but entirely one-sided. We have no replies. What we know of what she felt and thought, we know only from him. The poems they exchanged tell us little. It is perhaps unsurprising that she has come down to us in a pure, unsullied state, the kind and lifelong inspiration to a great man. There are questions; but they refer to him rather than to her. By contrast, the relationship with Vanessa is two-sided. She has a background and a lively character. She has never been a dependant. She commands attention within her family, and is unquestionably the dominant figure, not just over her younger siblings, but over her mother as well. She speaks up for herself, and a good deal of what she says is strong stuff which has had the unfortunate effect of giving her an almost threatening aspect in Swift's life. As a result, Vanessa has suffered an imprecise burden of blame, ostensibly for causing him trouble, when all she did was to assert a love in which he was also a willing partner.

It is difficult to deal independently with these two women, despite the fact that they led entirely separate lives and there is no recorded meeting between them. The reason is simple: Swift was emotionally involved with both of them. There is a marked contrast in the kind of emotion felt, but there can be no doubt of the depth and intensity of the feelings within each rela-tionship, and this creates problems which transcend the narrative.

Swift was 'in love' with Vanessa from the end of 1707 until her death in 1723, and this is a matter of record contained in their correspondence. Stella, who commanded a prominent position in his affairs during the same period, inspired in Swift a quite different form of love.[41] Something of the flavour of their rela-tionship may be surmised from the *Journal to Stella*.

'Pray, young women,' Swift writes on 25 December 1710, 'if I write so much as this every day, how will this paper hold a fortnight's work, and answer one of yours into the bargain? You never think of this, but let me go on like a simpleton. I wish you a merry Christmas, and many, many a one with poor Presto, at some pretty place.'[42] The following April he is responding to requests for shopping in London:

I have put the last commissions of MD [My Dears] in my account-book; but if there be any former ones, I have forgot them. I have Dingley's pocket-book down, and Stella's green silk apron, and the pound of tea; pray send me word if you have any other, and down they shall go. I will not answer your letter yet, saucy boxes. You are with the dean just now, madam Stella, losing your money. Why don't you name what numbers you have received? You say you have received my letters, but don't tell the number.[43]

And shortly afterwards: 'Stella jeers Presto for not coming over by Christmas; but indeed Stella does not jeer but reproach poor poor Presto. And how can I come away, and the First-Fruits not finished?'[44]

Swift was obsessively concerned about health, both his own and that of those dearest to him, and this is reflected throughout the *Journal*: 'I wish MD walked half as much as Presto. If I was with you, I'd make you walk; I would walk behind or before you, and you should have masks on, and be tucked up like any thing, and Stella is naturally a stout walker, and carries herself firm, methinks I see her strut, and step clever over a kennel; and Dingley would do well enough, if her petticoats were pinned up; but she is so embroiled, and so fearful, and then Stella scolds, and Dingley stumbles, and is so daggled. Have you got the whale-bone petticoats amongst you yet? I hate them; a woman here may hide a moderate gallant under them. Pshaw, what's all this I'm saying? methinks I am talking to MD face to face.'[45]

Not only was the *Journal to Stella* an 'invention' as a book, it was also the subject of much editorial alteration affecting in particular what is known as 'the little language' used by Swift in simulation of a way he, Stella and Rebecca Dingley talked together. 'Do you know what? When I am writing in our language I make up my mouth just as if I was speaking it. I caught myself at it just now.'[46] The two-volume Harold Williams edition of 1948 is authoritative in setting this right. He identifies, as far as is possible, the various abbreviated forms of address: 'Md' or 'MD' for My Dear or My Dears; 'Ppt' is Poppet or Poor Pretty Thing, and applies to Stella; 'D' or 'Dd' is Rebecca Dingley. Swift is known as 'Presto' from the Italian for his name, given him by the Duchess of Shrewsbury. He also uses 'Pdfr', pronounced Podefar and possibly meaning Poor dear foolish rogue, or Poor dear fellow. He uses the subscription FW as Farewell, but also possibly to mean Foolish Wenches. In addition to explaining, and in many cases restoring, the language and the forms of address of the original, Harold Williams also had to delete invented terms of endearment deriving from earlier editors, notably Swift's cousin, Deane Swift.

Swift was never 'in love' with Stella. A different word must be used to define the undoubtedly deep affection between the two. His feelings for her, placing her somewhere between niece and daughter, had become settled in the early years of the eighteenth century. We have no reason to doubt Swift's claim, in his letter to the Rev. William Tisdall, that, though he would have chosen marriage with Esther Johnson 'above all persons on earth' (this was more than three years before his first recorded encounter with Esther Van Homrigh), *conversation* with her was 'the utmost I ever gave way to'.[47] Nor have we reason to doubt the long-established view that Swift and Stella were never alone together. He did write her poems; but they are not love poems. When she and Dingley returned after their trip to London—probably to visit Martha Giffard and other family or friends from the Moor Park period—Swift rejoined them and returned to the life of parish work at Laracor and Church work in Dublin. With Stella, Swift seems always to have been happy, and to have enjoyed a friendship of lasting and growing value about which he wrote with deep emotion at the time of her death.

What of Rebecca Dingley? In the end she was the person who knew Swift longer than anyone else, and was probably privy to even more secrets than her much younger friend. Swift actually found Dingley something of a trial, as one might an awkward aunt; he referred to her on more than one occasion in terms critical of her intellectual abilities. But he was constant in the mixture of kindness and duty that coloured his actions towards her, right up to her death, which preceded his by only two years. Swift's relationship with Stella is inseparable from his relationship with Dingley; and in fact there is no letter extant written by Swift to Stella alone.

Our knowledge of this three-way relationship derives mainly from Swift's second sojourn in London, from the autumn of 1710 until the death of Queen Anne on 1 August 1714. During this period, in one of the greatest series of letters ever written, Swift kept an exact account of all the events in which he was involved on behalf of the Church of Ireland. His personal life (though he gives fewer details of his meetings with the Van Homrigh family than they deserve); his problems with servants; secrets about his writing and an interpretation of its impact; high matters of policy, involving the administration, the war machine, foreign governments, treaties and battles; even such details as the food he consumed, the daily state of his health, and the difficulty of writing in bed—all are related to these two women in Dublin. The record is a daily one, but the letters are compounded into accounts that cover upwards of a week. They have the vigour of immediacy, the truthfulness of a well-kept and well-written diary. In no small measure Swift is expressing his recognition that he was witness to a momentous period in history.

Supremely important, above all other descriptions, and also above the expression of feelings—which itself is the thread giving life to the correspondence— is the throng of people among whom Swift moves.

We are in the cockpit of power, with Robert Harley the chief engineer.[48] We witness at first hand his dealings with the Queen. We admire the skill in his handling of diplomacy and foreign policy, the war in Europe, the overweening arrogance of the commander of the Army, the Duke of Marlborough, the careful balancing of public opinion for and against the war, and the deployment of Swift in bringing about a significant change in attitude, sufficient to gain public approval for peace and the downfall of Marlborough.

Swift arrived in London in September 1710. Once again he was on Church business, his main, indeed at that point his only, purpose the remission of the First Fruits and Twentieth Parts. The Whig administration still ruled. Within days Swift presented himself to the outgoing Lord Treasurer, the Earl of Godolphin, who had already been asked by the Queen to break his staff,[49] and to Lord Somers, the Lord President. Swift was still nominally a Whig supporter, and was seen as such, not just in his political contacts, but in his literary ones as well. But power had slipped from the Whigs. The Tories were forming the Queen's new government. And if Swift were to achieve his objectives he had to redirect his energies towards the Tory leadership, which rested with Harley, and his closest deputy, Henry St John, later Viscount Bolingbroke.

Swift viewed the Whig leaders with increasing distrust anyway; they had failed him on his previous visits, and in general had given him little enough by way of preferment or satisfaction. Moreover, their latest mistake—the prosecution of Dr Henry Sacheverell, the High Church vicar of St Saviour's in Southwark, who had preached in St Paul's in defence of the special position of the Anglican Church—alienated Swift's sympathies, as it did those of the population more generally. Sacheverell, who in his sermon had attacked the Whig Junto and its leader, Godolphin, became a martyr, Queen Anne set in train the dismantling of her Whig ministry, and Swift found himself drawn into the Tory fold. He suffered as a result; aspersions were cast on him, as a turncoat motivated by self-interest. In fact he acted from conviction. He was opposed to the European war, on diplomatic and economic grounds. He was staunchly High Church; his experiences in Ireland, particularly Kilroot, made him an opponent of all Dissenters. And the Whigs had constantly frustrated his efforts on behalf of the Irish Church.

In Robert Harley he found a great conciliator. Harley came from a Whig background, and was essentially a moderate in all things. His greatest passion was collecting books, and it was said that his familiarity with his own enormous library was so intimate that if a title was named, no matter how obscure, he could find it immediately. He was a remarkable, and greatly underrated, politician, the father of the modern Cabinet system of government. He contrived an administration in turbulent times, and, working with a difficult monarch, transformed bellicose England into a forward-looking modern state, primarily concerned with profitable trade worldwide.

Robert Harley, first Earl of Oxford, by Godfrey Kneller

Swift achieved his principal objective early on. Harley gained for him the Queen's consent on the remission of dues to the Church in Ireland, bringing to an end the formal part of Swift's mission from Dublin. Harley spotted immediately the benefit he might derive from Swift's continued help, and gave him editorial control of *The Examiner*, which was the mouthpiece of the administration. Unlike Daniel Defoe, who also worked for Harley, Swift did so for no financial reward—though he certainly hoped for preferment in due course—but as a friend. And the friendship developed rapidly. Quite soon after Swift's arrival in London, letters which form the early part of the *Journal to Stella* talk of frequent dinner engagements at which he met other leading figures in the Tory party. He became particularly close to Erasmus Lewis, the powerful equivalent of today's Cabinet Secretary.

The business in hand concerned the war in Europe and the various attempts to conclude a peace. Far from being a matter of united state activity in pursuit of a broadly accepted national goal, this was in fact divisive, with the Whigs seeking to promote the war, under a leadership in which their principal figure, the Earl of Godolphin, was closely related to the Duke of Marlborough.

The Duchess of Marlborough had for many years enjoyed the favours of Queen Anne, whom she had known since the Queen was a young princess. But her position was usurped; she was disgraced and dismissed, and so began the gradual downfall of the

John Churchill, first Duke of Marlborough, by Godfrey Kneller, engraved by Pieter Tanje

Henry St John, Viscount Bolingbroke, by T. Murray, engraved by George White

Marlboroughs. Court intrigue, political manipulation, the journalistic brilliance of Swift in undermining the enemies of Harley, and the gradual but inevitable turning of British public opinion against the war in Europe, brought about a revolution in English history of momentous significance. Swift stood at the centre of these events, and recounted them in the *Journal to Stella* in vivid and intimate language.

Harley shortly became Earl of Oxford, an honour not immediately duplicated in the case of his close rival in the Tory party, Henry St John, who was kept in the Commons on account of his brilliant debating powers there. This began a split which was to prove fatal within three years. Much of Swift's energy, reported in the *Journal*, was spent on reconciling the differences between the two men, one of them Lord Treasurer, the other Secretary of State. But Swift's primary task was to change opinion about the war in Europe, and this he achieved in one of his greatest literary feats, *The Conduct of the Allies*, published on 27 November 1711. As well as discrediting the whole idea of the war, it also damned the Duke of Marlborough, claiming he was engaged in self-advancement and financial corruption. Though the road to eventual peace was still long and tortuous, the direction was firmly set by these events. The Peace of Utrecht was signed on 11 April 1713.

There are many mentions in the *Journal* of Swift's literary life and of his contacts with other writers. He tells of visiting Congreve, 'who is almost blind with cataracts growing on his eyes ... and besides he is never rid of the gout, yet he looks young and fresh, and is as cheerful as ever. He is younger by three years or more than I, and I am twenty years younger than he. He gave me a pain in the great toe, by mentioning the gout. I find such suspicions frequently, but they go off again.'[50] The tone here is so different from that adopted when Swift was Temple's amanuensis, contemplating lines for Congreve the successful playwright. Ten years later, when Swift was confined to Ireland, John Gay wrote to tell him: 'Mr. Congreve I see often. He always mentions you with the strongest expressions of esteem and friendship. He labours still under the same afflictions, as to his sight and gout, but in his intervals of health, he has not lost anything of his cheerful temper. I passed all the last season with him at the Bath ...'[51]

John Arbuthnot (1667–1735), Physician-in-Ordinary to Queen Anne from 1709 until her death, was a friend of Swift's at this time. He was a Scot who had studied medicine at St Andrew's University, settling then in London. Also a friend of Pope, he wrote a *History of John Bull*, as well as contributing largely to *Memoirs of Martinus Scriblerus*.

Swift expected a bishopric for his services to the State. Instead he got the deanery of St Patrick's Cathedral in Dublin. He was installed there in June 1713, and returned to London in September. The later part of his years in London were marred by the growing division between Harley and St John (who had become Viscount Bolingbroke in 1712), by his own ill-health—he suffered from labyrinthine vertigo, or Ménière's Disease, as well as having a severe attack of shingles—and by the disappointment of his preferment, which he thought was less than he deserved. Everyone connected with the Harley administration became somewhat depressed by the approach of Queen Anne's death and the Hanoverian

James Butler, second Duke of Ormonde, by Godfrey Kneller, engraved by J. Smith

accession, which would bring about a return of the Whigs to power.

One of the casualties was the second Duke of Ormonde (1665–1746). During both of Swift's periods in London, the Duke had been Lord Lieutenant. He returned to take the place of the Duke of Marlborough after his disgrace and dismissal, thereby incurring the enmity of the Whigs. He flirted with Jacobitism, and was dismissed after the accession of George I. He was liked by Swift, but had no talent for politics or public affairs. Swift comments on him: 'The duke of Ormond is censured here by those in power for very wrong management in the affair of the mayoralty. He is governed by fools; and has usually much more sense than his advisers, but never proceeds by it.'[52] He was conscious of the Duke's power, however: 'You know the Deanry is in the D. Ormonds gift, but this is concerted between the Qu[een,] Ld Tr [Harley], & D. Ormd, to make room for me. I do not know whethr it will yet be done, some unlucky Accident may yet come; neither can I feel Joy at passing my days in Ireld: and I confess I thought the Ministry would not let me go; but perhaps thy cant help it.'[53]

The wide diversity of content, and the frequent complexities of the narrative, as it shifts between politics, literature, social life and personal expressions of affection, in no way impair *Journal to Stella*'s overall appeal as one of the greatest exercises in diary or letter writing in the English language. Swift clearly intended it to have an overall coherence, and he used it later to write a history of the last four years of Queen Anne's reign, a history which he was advised not to publish, and which only appeared many years later. In casting his eyes over the intimate writing of these letters he clearly failed to translate their brilliant perceptions and wide social and human grasp to the less familiar ends of historical writing. The letters stand as a unique testament to the man's vigour and

sanity, his judgment and skill, his wit and outspoken-
ness. They are also a tribute to the two women he was
addressing. They were his family, free to know his
mind as no one else did.

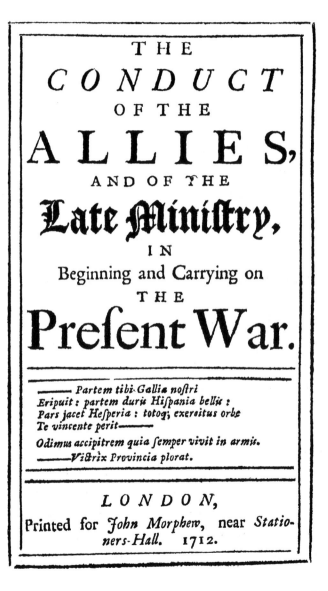

THE

CONDUCT

OF THE

ALLIES,

AND OF THE

𝕷𝖆𝖙𝖊 𝕸𝖎𝖓𝖎𝖘𝖙𝖗𝖞,

IN

Beginning and Carrying on

THE

Prefent War.

——— *Partem tibi Gallia noftri*
Eripuit: partem duris Hifpania bellis:
Pars jacet Hefperia: totoq; exercitus orbe
Te vincente perit———
Odimus accipitrem quia femper vivit in armis.
———*Victrix Provincia plorat.*

LONDON,
Printed for *John Morphew*, near *Statio-*
ners-Hall. 1712.

St Patrick's Cathedral, Dublin, engraved by Isaac Taylor

VI

Dean of St Patrick's

On the accession of George I, the Tory administration was replaced, inaugurating a long period of Whig rule. Swift returned to Dublin, his world in pieces. The long and increasingly bitter rivalry between his two great political friends, Lord Oxford and Viscount Bolingbroke, which had come near to splitting the Tory party, had ended with Oxford retiring to his country estate, having narrowly missed impeachment and possible imprisonment, and with Bolingbroke fleeing to France, the suspicion of Jacobitism like a thundercloud over his head. Swift himself felt he was going into exile. As an ally of the Tories, and one who had done great damage to Whig interests, he was a marked man. The royal patent appointing him to the deanship of St Patrick's Cathedral was a precious and immensely important docu-

King George I, by D. Stevens, mezzotint by John Faber the Younger, left, and Archbishop William King of Dublin, by R. Tighe, etched by K. O'Hara

ment. But it was a political reward, not based on any decision of the Chapter of the Cathedral, and this added to the sense of frustrated ambition. He was answerable to Archbishop King, under whose direction he had gone to London. King was no friend; he was fair, but authoritarian, and he viewed the Swift stripped of powerful political friends in a different light. For some time to come, after his return to the city of his birth, Swift, perhaps not surprisingly, walked a cautious and vulnerable path.

He found that as Dean his powers were more circumscribed than he had anticipated. He devoted his time once again to his living at Laracor. He had promised, if given preferment, to hand it on to

Anthony Raymond, who held a living in nearby Trim. But he could not part with it, and perhaps on the understanding that by 'preferment' he meant a position in England, he held Laracor until his death.

He was not well. For more than a year he had suffered from indifferent health, much of it almost certainly deriving from, or associated with, the stresses of his political work. He was beset by trivial but intensely irritating problems. He had to sort out, even clean out, the Deanery. He had to do much the same with the Cathedral. Obsessed with cleanliness all his life, he found that his predecessor, John Stearne, had left both places in a poor state. He wanted, or needed, to change the Cathedral choir; appointments had been made for non-musical reasons, and although Swift had no taste for singing himself, he did value excellence in work and behaviour.

The overriding worry, however, was the domestic one. His return to Dublin had not been satisfactorily welcomed by Stella; there was a lack of warmth for a time. Swift had been away for nearly four years. During that period he had formed so close a relationship with Vanessa that within months of his return to Dublin she followed him. Ostensibly she came to deal with property interests, but as her letters show, she was more and more deeply in love with Swift and determined to hold him to their mutual emotional commitments. The passion was firm as ever after six years' residence back in Dublin, as may be seen in brief extracts from two letters from Vanessa to Swift in 1720:

Put my passion under the utmost restraint, send me as distant from you as the earth will allow, yet you cannot banish those charming ideas, which will ever stick by me whilst I have the use of memory. Nor is the love I bear you only seated in my soul, for there is not a single atom of my frame that is not blended with it.

I was born with violent passions, which terminate all in one —that unexpressible passion I have for you.[54]

Vanessa had a fine house on the river Liffey at Celbridge. Though much altered, it still stands, in grounds that are much as they were then. She demanded visits; he declined. She berated him about his neglect; he compromised over his feelings, and over the very real difficulties he would confront if he openly carried on a liaison with her. He clearly prevaricated also over visits and encounters in Dublin, where she had a town house. They met, they corresponded, there was a perpetual element of risk and embarrassment; in short they behaved as lovers, and there is no reason to suppose that two people as scrupulously honest in their feelings as Swift and Vanessa did not put into practice the yearnings which are to be found in the letters they exchanged.

A great deal has been written about Stella during this period. Virtually all of it is speculative. We know from her nothing of her views on the circumstances surrounding Swift in respect of Vanessa, and we know virtually nothing from Swift himself. Our contemporary and later sources are grounded in rumour, much of it clearly mistaken. All three parties to the relationship—Rebecca Dingley included—wanted to protect their way of life. Undoubtedly, Swift's own behaviour operated to this end. He wanted no scandal. It could prejudice his standing in the Church; at worst it could cost him his position as Dean.

Stella is often seen solely in the Swift context. But she had a life of her own, friends, activities, property, standing. She could be solemn and grave, sociable, playful and witty. In the early period after Swift's return an adjustment needed to take place. It was followed by greater harmony and the restoration of the former friendship. This prevailed from then on.

Swift took to riding for the sake of his health, and travelled through the countryside of Ireland, stopping with friends and acquaintances. These trips sometimes lasted for two or three months. He wrote letters all the time. He kept up a correspondence with literary and political friends in England, at times with an eye on the remote possibility of a return of Tory rule, at times with the desire for help from friends, Addison among them, in improving his position. He wrote a good deal of verse, and began work on *Gulliver's Travels*.

By 1720, with Swift in his fifty-third year, uncertainty seemed to have prevailed in almost every department of his life. The gifted pamphleteer remained silent. The satirist uttered no spleen or invective, railed against no foolishness, made no mark at all upon his time. The poet indulged in what he described to Charles Ford as 'panegyrics', which in fact included a good deal of limp material addressed to Stella or dealing in a supposedly philosophic way with women more generally, or simply with experiences. The total output of the period occupies but a small percentage of his overall achievement as a poet.

Then, in 1720, he appears to have reconciled himself to the fact that the rest of his life would be spent in Ireland. He judged as negligible the chances of a Tory return to power, and probably recognized that even if it happened he would no longer have any role to play. The business of politics itself had passed beyond the intimate, pamphlet-driven persuasions of the early years of the century. The Whigs had redirected the processes of power, and with the failure of the Jacobite threat the main emphasis was on domestic and international trade.

It was precisely in this area that Swift now saw an opportunity for himself. He wrote a highly political essay, *A Proposal for the Universal Use of Irish Manufacture*. Yet it was not political in the old sense of the word. As an Irish leader of thought and political action, Swift transcended party at a stroke. He was no longer a Tory attacking the Whigs. He was an Irishman defending local interests against the centralist oppression of the Parliament in Westminster. In this respect he did more than merely transcend the old politics. He achieved a metamorphosis of himself, shifting the foundations of his life, perhaps a trifle reluctantly and with nostalgic glances over his shoulder, from an ambivalent Dublin–London axis, to a singular focus on Ireland's interests. The countryside around Dublin, indeed throughout Ireland, was impoverished. The weaving industry, which was centred near the deanery, was particularly badly hit by the import of English cloths. Dublin offered unnerving scenes of want and destitution.

With certain precise exceptions, notable among them the publication of the main work he was engaged on at the time, *Gulliver's Travels*, Swift had reorganized his life for the future, and created a new impetus for what he knew and loved best, the pamphleteer's disruption of complacency, corruption and chicanery. At the same time, he cast *A Proposal* in terms of obedience, respect, even love, for the monarch, George I. The pamphlet, scheduled to appear on the King's birthday, contains the wish: 'I hope and believe, nothing could please his majesty better than to hear that his loyal subjects of both sexes in this kingdom celebrated his birthday (now approaching) universally clad in their own manufacture.'

Not surprisingly, grave exception was taken to *A Proposal*. The printer was prosecuted; in the trial the judge sent the jurors back no fewer than nine times in order to obtain a guilty verdict, and what he got was effectively a 'special verdict' amounting to a direction for retrial. It was even put forward, as part of the bench's own prosecution, that the pamphlet was 'Jacobite' in its real intentions. The underlying reality was that Swift, who was of course seen as behind the work, had obtained the crucial public support which was his best protection against authority's spleen.

Swift was back in business as a campaigner, and not before time. His first significant pamphlet in six years was followed two years later by the first of his great series of *Drapier's Letters*. He was unique as a protagonist in fighting this particular battle. He knew the ground better than anyone, and he recognized that his singular skill was uniquely appropriate to the intimacies of public life in Ireland, and particularly in Dublin. He could wage a solitary war through the exercise of his pen, and he had already demonstrated his capacity to win.

The *Drapier's Letters* were occasioned by an attempt to impose Wood's Halfpence on the Irish population. Wood was an English entrepreneur who was given a patent for the introduction of a base-metal coinage, solely in Ireland. The scheme would have required the surrender of the coinage of the realm, including gold and silver, in exchange for the new money, which was worthless elsewhere. Swift saw the fundamental and irreversible damage which this threatened to the people of Ireland, and took up his pen on their behalf. The *Letters* were a sustained cry for the commercial and economic independence of the Irish people, which Swift was to summarize in due course in *A Short View of the State of Ireland*, where he says: 'Ireland is the only Kingdom I ever heard or read of, either in ancient or modern history, which was denied the liberty of exporting their native commodities and manufactures wherever they pleased ...'

Though the case has been made that a new coinage was indeed needed, Wood's Halfpence was a vile scheme, both in conception and execution, and deserved rigorous opposition. But the state was slow

John Carteret, first Earl Granville, by Godfrey Kneller, mezzotint by P. Pelham

to act. The Lord Lieutenant, the Duke of Grafton, was already compromised in Wood's interest before his arrival in Ireland. The Chancellor of the Exchequer and First Lord of the Treasury, Robert Walpole was also on Wood's side, and his government procrastinated, Wood himself continuing to push strongly for the implementation of the patent he had been granted. Fears grew in Ireland that the people would be steadily deprived of all their gold in exchange for a base-metal currency. But the growing sense of outrage lacked sufficient focus until Swift's first letter.

The controversy lasted for two years and was finally resolved by the Duke of Grafton's successor, Lord Carteret. He and Swift respected each other. There is a fine and rousing description, in Thomas Sheridan's *Life of Dr Swift*, of Swift confronting Carteret with an explosive denunciation to which the Lord Lieutenant had the wisdom and tact to reply with a quotation from Vergil. It must have been an exciting encounter to witness.

Ten years after his ignominious return to Ireland in 1714, Swift was a national hero. He preserved this position until the end of his life. The achievement of this ran side by side with sustained private difficulties. Swift's relationship with Vanessa was increasingly turbulent from the time of her return to Ireland until her death. Her mother died before she departed from London. Her younger brother, Ginkel, died in childhood; the older brother, Bartholomew, who was a friend of Swift's friend, Charles Ford, also died young. Her sister, Moll, joined her in the house in Celbridge, suffering from consumption, and died there in 1721. Vanessa herself, probably contracting the same killer disease as a result of nursing the younger woman, became ill in 1723 and died in June.

Swift went into the country after her death on a protracted journey lasting some months. It is difficult to piece together convincingly the events surrounding the last days of their relationship. Our view is coloured by a great deal of gossip, and by some hard facts which suggest a degree of indifference on the part of both of them. He apparently became impatient of her importunities and insensitive about her appeals for kindness. She made no mention of Swift in her will.

Of the death of Stella we know more. He mentions her ill-health in letters, and her death, five years after that of Vanessa, was both public and solemn. Her coffin rested in the Cathedral, across from the Deanery. The funeral service was there, and she was buried beneath its floor. Swift wrote movingly of her life, describing her qualities and virtues, her appearance, her sense of humour and her courage.

'She was sickly from her childhood until about the age of fifteen; but then grew into perfect health, and was looked upon as one of the most beautfiul, graceful, and agreeable young women in London, only a little too fat. Her hair was blacker than a raven, and every feature of her face in perfection.' He wrote at her death, paused for a night or so, and then wrote again:

This is the night of the funeral, which my sickness will not suffer me to attend. It is now nine at night; and I am removed into another apartment, that I may not see the light in the church, which is just over against the window of my bed-chamber. With all the softness of temper that became a lady, she had the personal courage of a hero ... She never had the least absence of mind in conversation, nor given to interruption, or appeared eager to put in her word, by waiting impatiently until another had done. She spoke in a most agreeable voice, in the plainest words, never hesitating, except out of modesty before new faces, where she was somewhat reserved; nor, among her nearest friends, ever spoke much at a time.[55]

Jonathan Swift, by C. Jarvis (sic, recte Jervas), engraved by P. Fourdrinier

VII

Gulliver

Swift followed the recovery of his name in Ireland with an even more resounding triumph in England, the publication of *Travels into Several Remote Nations of the World* in 1727. *Gulliver's Travels*, as the book came to be called, was an immediate success, read by everyone 'from the cabinet council to the nursery'. Here was satire, and hidden meanings; a series of stories, graduating from the light to the dark, from the relatively simple worlds of Lilliput and Brobdingnag to the complex philosophy and science of Laputa, and then the black reversal of behaviour among the Houyhnhnms.

The simplest of the abiding images is a paradox of scale: How can a man who bestrides the world like a colossus in one part be reduced to pigmy proportions in another? If Swift looked back over his career, this is what had happened to him. He had been raised up and cast down. He had transcended his humble origins, literally to walk beside the monarch, to give advice and direction to those in power, and then to fall from grace. In Ireland he had gone through a similar transition, raising himself to a remarkable public acclaim and reverence from a position near to vilification. The vanity of human ambition is the object of Swift's satire just as it is part of his experience. And his masterly narrative reveals life at two different courts, in the world of academic and scientific inquiry, and finally in the world of a supposed 'nature', where man and animal are reversed in their representation of nobility and bestiality. It is this which in the end horrifies and disgusts Lemuel Gulliver.

Swift still had much to say, some of it frivolous, some serious. He went back to journalism with his weekly paper, *The Intelligencer*, compiled in collaboration with Thomas Sheridan. It contained brief essays on circumstances of daily life, and poems. It had no serious or sustained political direction or purpose, though it did touch on party politics. At the same time it was inspired by social concern at the poverty of the people. Its content was lively and provocative, but it did not flourish. What is perhaps best of all about it is the fact that these two close friends were able to indulge together their love of language games and puns, on which Sheridan, no less than Swift, had expended a great deal of energy.

In the following year, 1729, appeared perhaps Swift's best-known pamphlet, *A Modest Proposal for*

Thomas Sheridan, engraved by Cook

Preventing the Children of Poor People from being a Bur-then to their Parents. Its economy of statement and masterful simplicity of argument has separated it from the reality which it was meant to reflect, that of a country exploited by wealth but riven from end to end by the most abject poverty. Swift at this stage was a widely travelled man, closely in touch with Irish affairs, and still productive in his writing of a wide and magisterial set of judgments about the wrongs with which he felt the people of Ireland were surrounded.

St Patrick's Hospital, Dublin, from an original drawing by John Aheron

Swift did not shrink from apportioning a good deal of the blame for the state of the country on the people of the country. But his concern was strengthened rather than compromised by this. If he could not persuade, he would shame people into changing their own fortunes. Satire had this purpose, no matter where its words were directed. This was as true of Swift's output of poetry in these years as it was of the prose works about Ireland. The poems vary; there is that infamous group which cast a satiric if not vulgar eye on women, stripping them down physically to the real body beneath. And there are many finer late works, culminating in his last major poem, 'The Legion Club'.

It is difficult to chart the final decade of Swift's life without feelings of compassion for the man as his

Jonathan Swift, by R. Barber, etched by B. Wilson

health steadily declined, his friends died, and his fre-
netic energy continued to pour forth words. He was
celebrated and admired. His birthdays were occasions
for public rejoicing. And his death, in 1745, was an
occasion for national mourning. He left his wealth for
the foundation of St Patrick's Hospital, 'for the recep-
tion of ... Idiots and Lunaticks'.[56] He left also a boun-
tiful literary heritage. No Irishman has inspired as
prodigious a fund of folklore and legend, with the
possible exception of Daniel O'Connell. Swift the
writer has cast his shadow across poetry and drama,
politics and protest. He was that human rarity, an
honest and a brave man.

Acknowledgments

This short Life of Jonathan Swift was written to coincide with the Tenth International Congress on the Enlightenment, held in Dublin, 25–31 July 1999. At an early stage in the planning of that event the National Library of Ireland agreed to put on an exhibition about Swift and his contemporaries, with the emphasis on his life and his friends rather than on his writings. Radio Telefís Éireann subsequently commissioned a documentary about Swift. These three events—book, exhibition and documentary film—share a common theme and purpose. They reflect my own views on Swift and recognize that in the events of his life there remain many unresolved questions.

I would like to thank particularly Andrew Carpenter, whose guidance and support in writing the book was considerable. Research for it was carried out by

Helen Moss, whose work in the vast field of material on Swift and his period has been of inestimable value to me. Brendan O'Donoghue, Director of the National Library of Ireland, responded with immediate enthusiasm to the idea of an exhibition, and has been very helpful, together with members of his staff, Catherine Fahy, Colette O'Daly, Donal O'Luanaigh, Sylvia Lynam, John Farrell, Hyder Abbas, Sandra McDermott and Anita Joyce. For all three projects we borrowed from the National Gallery of Ireland, and I would like to thank the Board of Governors and Guardians for their permission, and Marie Bourke, Marie McFeely, Elizabeth Player and Niamh McGuinne for their practical help. Muriel McCarthy, Librarian of Marsh's Library, was very helpful, as were the administration staff of St Patrick's Cathedral, and of the Deanery. In particular I would like to thank the Dean-elect, the Right Reverend Robert McCarthy, and Kate Manning, the archivist. I was also helped by Dr Anthony Clare, Medical Director of St Patrick's Hospital. David Woolley has been supportive of this work, and I was helped by the Reverend Victor Griffin, Joe McMinn and Bob Mahony.

I owe a special debt to Maeve Binchy and Tony Sweeney, to Andrew Bonar Law, Jane Fenlon, Marie-Therese Nasmyth, Hermann Real, Robert Folkenflik and Maurice Craig. Jonathan Williams has been a help to the project, and to me. I am also grateful to Caxton Prints, Grosvenor Prints, Joslyn McDiarmuid, and Mr and Mrs Berkeley of Berkeley Castle. I am very much in the debt of Virginia Cardwell Moore and Polly Hutchison, and also Mandy O'Connell for help with research. Antony Farrell of the Lilliput Press accepted a tight schedule for the book and was an enthusiast for its content; Brendan Barrington edited it with an astonishing grasp of difficult material and great skill in accommodating my arguments while at the same time pressing his own. In terms of the overall project I would also like to thank Ian Graham, Tim Lawless, Brendan Campbell, Patricia Roche, Joe Mulholland, Mike Kelly, Fintan Ryan, Eamon Hayes, Martin O'Brien, Jean Feeney, Oonagh Young, Michael Kenny, Brother Finian at Celbridge Abbey, Mary O'Brien and Tony Adderley, Bill Simpson, Librarian, Trinity College Library, Ian Ross of the English Department at Trinity, Patricia Moriarty and Liam Belton of the Royal Hibernian Academy, Superintendant John Mulderrig and Sergeant Martin Pelo of Kevin Street Garda Station, and Tony O'Shaughnessy at Dublin Castle.

Further Reading

Ball, F. Elrington, ed. *The Correspondence of Jonathan Swift, D.D.*, in six volumes (London, 1910). The first full and scholarly edition of the letters by a distinguished Irish scholar whose work paved the way for twentieth-century Swift studies. Superseded by the Harold Williams edition, in five volumes, incorporating additional letters, it is now in the process of being superseded again by an edition in four volumes, edited by David Woolley and published by Peter Lang, Frankfurt, 1999.

Ball, F. Elrington. *Swift's Verse: An Essay* (London, 1929). A good general account of Swift's poetry sensibly relating it to his life, and charting the growth and development of both his mind and his technique.

Craik, Henry. *The Life of Jonathan Swift, Dean of St Patrick's, Dublin*, in two volumes, second edition (London, 1984). Craik follows in Forster's footsteps, completing the unfinished task of the Life from 1711 on, and dealing with many difficult issues, including the writer's health.

Davis, Herbert, ed. *Prose Works of Jonathan Swift*, in fourteen volumes (Oxford, 1939–69). The most modern scholarly edition of Swift's works.

Delany, Patrick. *Observations upon Lord Orrery's Remarks on the Life and Writings of Dr Jonathan Swift* (London, 1754). As the title suggest, Delany, who was Swift's friend, attempts to correct and counter the generally adverse treatment of Swift by Orrery.

Donoghue, Denis. *Jonathan Swift: A Critical Introduction* (Cambridge, 1969). A complete critical survey of Swift's output, relating it firmly to the author's life and experience, and to his responses to the world he lived in.

Elias, A.C. *Swift at Moor Park: Problems in Biography and Criticism* (Philadelphia, 1982). The most comprehensive and scholarly account of the vitally important working relationship between Jonathan Swift and William Temple at Temple's home in Farnham, Surrey.

Ehrenpreis, Irvin. *Swift: The Man, His Works, and the Age*, in three volumes, second edition (London, 1983). Magisterial in intent, this substantial Life is at times heavy going.

Foot, Michael. *The Pen & the Sword* (London, 1957). The best account of Swift and the Tories during the period 1710–14, bringing to life the way in which power is exercised by politicians through journalists.

Forster, John. *The Life of Jonathan Swift*, Volume 1 (London, 1875). The author did not live to complete this work, but made a major contribution in terms of new and detailed research, giving us the first 'modern' biography.

Freeman, A. Martin, ed. *Vanessa and Her Correspondence with Jonathan Swift* (London, 1921). The first publication of the exchange of correspondence between Swift and Esther Van Homrigh, together with a sensible introduction about the relationship. The correspondence is clearly incomplete.

Johnston, Denis. *In Search of Swift* (Dublin, 1959). A key work in dealing with the controversies that have surrounded Swift. Johnston investigates Swift's possible illegitimacy, his relationships with Stella and Vanessa, and the position of Jonathan Swift the Elder in the King's Inns.

Le Brocquy, Sybil. *Cadenus* (Dublin, 1962). Important contributions are contained in this and other works by the same author, who investigated the Van Homrigh family petition to the House of Lords.

Longe, Julia, ed. *Martha, Lady Giffard: Life & Letters 1664–1722* (London, 1911). Throws light on the relationship between Swift and the Temple family after the death of Sir William Temple.

Mahony, Robert. *Jonathan Swift: The Irish Identity* (New Haven and London, 1995). A valuable account of how Swift's life and work have been seen in the period since his death, in Ireland, England and elsewhere.

McMinn, Joseph. *Jonathan's Travels: Swift and Ireland* (Belfast and New York, 1994). Swift travelled widely in Ireland on horseback, usually accompanied by a servant and staying with friends. He was away from Dublin for long periods, and this is an account of the effect of his travels on his life and work.

Nokes, David. *Jonathan Swift: A Hypocrite Reversed* (Oxford, 1985). The best modern single-volume Life of Swift.

Orrery, John, Earl of. *Remarks on the Life and Writings of Dr Jonathan Swift* (London, 1752). A gossipy and scandalous Life of Swift, the first to appear after his death. It had enormous circulation, and began the process of claim and counter-claim about the events of Swift's life.

Smith, David Nichols. *The Letters of Jonathan Swift to Charles Ford* (Oxford, 1935). The letters reveal an important and sustained relationship expressed in intimate terms, supporting the theory that the two men were related.

Swift, Deane. *An Essay upon the Life, Writings, and Character, of Dr Jonathan Swift* (London, 1755). Deane Swift, cousin of Jonathan, was one of those who sought to straighten out the misleading claims and assertions made by Orrery. To some extent he made the situation worse.

Thompson, Paul V. and Dorothy Jay, eds. *The Account Books of Jonathan Swift* (Newark and London, 1984). An invaluable source book about Swift's day-to-day life as recorded in his own account books.

Williams, Harold, ed. *Jonathan Swift: Journal to Stella*, in two volumes (Oxford, 1948). The scholarly edition of the *Journal*, restoring the true test, and with an excellent introduction.

Williams, Harold, ed. *The Poems of Jonathan Swift*, in three volumes, second edition (Oxford, 1958). The best edition of the poems.

Woodbridge, Homer E. *Sir William Temple: The Man and His Work* (New York and London, 1940). The best account of Temple's life and work.

Notes

INTRODUCTION

1 *The Correspondence of Jonathan Swift, D.D.*, 6 vols, edited by F. Elrington Ball (London, 1910), Vol. III, pp. 330–1. The full epitaph, still visible in St Mary's Church, Warwick, reads: 'Fulke Greville, servant to Queen Elizabeth, councillor to King James, and friend to Sir Philip Sidney. Tropaeum Peccati.'

I SWIFT'S UPBRINGING

2 Irvin Ehrenpreis, *Swift: The Man, His Works, and the Age*, 3 vols, second edition (London, 1983), I, p. 52.

3 Quoted in Constantia E. Maxwell, *A History of Trinity College* (Dublin, 1946), p. 74.

4 The quote is from Ehrenpreis, I, p. 49. For a fuller account of Marsh in these respects, see Ehrenpreis, I, pp. 48–50.

II MOOR PARK

5 'Autobiographical Fragment', in Herbert Davis, ed., *Jonathan Swift: Miscellaneous and Autobiographical Pieces* (Oxford, 1969), p. 193. For detailed consideration of the 'Autobiographical Fragment', see Denis Johnston, *In Search of Swift* (Dublin, 1959).

6 Sir William Temple to Sir Robert Southwell, 29 May 1690. Ball, I, p. 2.

7   Deane Swift, *An Essay upon the Life, Writings, and Character, of Dr Jonathan Swift* (London, 1775), p. 38.

8   For details on this and other poems, see Harold Williams, ed., *The Poems of Jonathan Swift*, second edition, 3 vols (Oxford, 1958). See also Homer E. Woodbridge, *Sir William Temple* (New York and London, 1940), particularly p. 219. The Ode was first published by Richard Dodsley in 1745, in the tenth volume of the *Miscellanies*. It has been in the *Works* ever since. Scholars have argued over the date and place of its composition. As poetry it has been treated dismissively, as juvenilia; as a biographical source it has been largely ignored.

9   Ball, I, p. 1, n. 4.

10 'Autobiographical Fragment', p. 193.

11 In a correction to the Cobbe copy of the 'Autobiographical Fragment', recorded by Denis Johnston, Swift changes the date of his journey to Ireland, further frustrating those trying to sort out this difficult period. Johnston writes (p. 117): 'The fact that he could not say simply that he was given a job with Southwell that came to nothing, must be bound up with some unpleasantness about the incident, that he does not wish to remember.' This interpretation is open to question.

12 Temple to Southwell, 29 May 1690. Ball, I, p. 2.

13 Quoted in Williams, I, p. 14, from Ball, I, p. 363. The reference comes from a long letter of 1692 to his cousin Thomas Swift in which Swift gives details of his method of writing at the time.

14 Pindar, the Greek lyric poet (*c.* 522–442 BC), used many forms of verse, his Olympian odes being both formal and florid, with exaggerated expression, suited to the celebration of victories, either military or sporting. Abraham Cowley (1618–67), who was Swift's more recent model, brought the loose prosodic structure to a high level of perfection. Swift never matches Cowley's economy of thought and wit. Instead, he seems to romp, with all the enjoyment and enthusiasm of youth, within the frame which Cowley perfected.

15 Ehrenpreis is unnecessarily dismissive of the work of the Society, and sees 'timidity and diffidence' in Swift's attitude: 'Swift dared not follow his own literary schemes but looked to Temple and Lady Giffard for hints.' There is no evidence for this. Both the letter and the Ode suggest the opposite. Ehrenpreis's analysis of the Ode itself is valuable.

16 Swift to Kendall, 11 February 1692. Ball, I, p. 4. Kendall was

vicar of Thornton, ten miles from Leicester. His wife was sister to Swift's mother.

17 Swift to Thomas Swift, 6 December 1693. Ball, I, pp. 367–8.

18 'Autobiographical Fragment', p. 194.

19 Martha Giffard to Lady Betty Berkeley, 30 December [?1697]. See *Martha, Lady Giffard: Life & Letters 1664–1722*, edited by Julia Longe (London, 1911), p. 216.

20 Quoted in Ehrenpreis, I, p. 148.

21 Quoted in Ehrenpreis, I, p. 152.

22 The view is endorsed by Homer Woodbridge, specifically in respect of the letter to Sir Robert Southwell. See Woodbridge, *Sir William Temple*, pp. 220, 333. In general, biographers ignore what they cannot explain, but several, from Henry Craik to Irvin Ehrenpreis, have inferred a transient status for Swift at Moor Park which the present writer finds difficult to accept.

23 See Ehrenpreis, I, pp. 186–7, for a more detailed analysis. There is, of course, a huge literature on this crucial work in Swift's evolution as a writer.

24 Swift to Jane Waring, 29 April 1696. Ball, I, p. 18.

25 Sir Walter Scott, ed., *Works of Jonathan Swift*, I, p. 51.

III BETWEEN IRELAND AND ENGLAND

26 Ehrenpreis, II, p. 8.

27 *The Prose Works of Jonathan Swift, D.D.*, Vol. I, London, 1897, xcii.

28 Ball, I, pp. 33–4.

29 According to Denis Johnston's useful log, between May 1701 and autumn 1705 Swift made eight sea-crossings, of a total of twenty-six in his lifetime. During this period of frequent coming and going he spent a total of roughly twenty-nine months in Ireland and twenty-four in England. Thereafter, he spent longer periods in Ireland until the long stay in England from 1710 to 1713. See Johnston, *In Search of Swift*, pp. 133–4.

30 F. Elrington Ball, *Swift's Verse: An Essay* (London, 1929), p. 64. Thomas Herbert, eighth Earl of Pembroke (1656–1733), served as First Lord of the Admiralty, Lord Privy Seal, Lord High Admiral (on two occasions), and President of the Royal Society.

IV SPILLED COFFEE AND FIRST FRUITS

31 He wrote her love letters at various times until her death in 1723. She replied with passionate letters of her own. There are

forty-five surviving letters between them, and from internal evidence it has been conservatively estimated that at least that many have been lost. In addition, there are periods of time (1714–19, 1720–2) when a whole section of correspondence may have existed, but is now lost. There is no evidence in the existing letters to suggest that these gaps represent any break in their relationship. It was constant, stormy, and, in the end, heartbreaking for her, and probably for him as well. Of the forty-five letters referred to above, Vanessa is responsible for seventeen, Swift for twenty-eight. It is Swift, not Vanessa, who writes the greater number of letters at the end of their correspondence, and at no time does he seek to terminate their relationship or the exchange of letters.

32 Swift to Vanessa, 4 August 1720, in *Vanessa and Her Correspondence with Jonathan Swift*, edited by A. Martin Freeman (London, 1921), p. 121. Swift attempts the listing of past events in two further letters to Vanessa, that of 1 June 1722 (p. 133), and at the end of his last surviving letter to her, of 17 August 1722 (p. 144).

33 *Cadenus and Vanessa* was first published in 1726. The poem is a lightly disguised account of the relationship between Swift and Vanessa, located in classical setting and telling of a middle-aged man and a much younger woman who fall in love. There were numerous editions in that year, in Dublin and London, with variations in the text, including the presence or absence of the lines beginning 'But what Success ...' which refer to the extent of the love between the two. See *Poems*, edited by Harold Williams, second edition (Oxford, 1958), Vol. II, pp. 683–714. Williams give an excellent account of the publishing history of the poem, including reference to the widespread circulation of manuscript copies.

34 See *The Account Books of Jonathan Swift*, transcribed and with an Introduction by Paul V. Thompson and Dorothy Jay Thompson (Newark and London, 1984).

35 Swift to Vanessa, 1 June 1722, in Freeman, p. 135.

36 The Kit-Cat Club was a Whig institution. Among its members was Lord Wharton, who presented a goblet engraved with verses to Anne Long on her beauty.

37 Ball dates the *Decree* between the end of December 1707 and the beginning of January 1708; Ehrenpreis suggests New Year's Day 1708. It was first printed in a miscellany entitled *Letters*,

Poems, and Tales: Amorous, Satyrical, and Gallant. Which passed between Several Persons of Distinction (London, 1718).

38 Deane Swift, *An Essay Upon the Life, Writings, and Character, of Dr Jonathan Swift*, p. 131.

39 This *nom-de-plume*, though invented by Swift, was later used by Richard Steele, when he started *The Tatler*, in 1709.

V 'JOURNAL TO STELLA'

40 It was not until later that the collection which Sheridan called *Journal to Stella* appeared as a separate volume, and it has been treated by editors of Swift ever since in what is, in certain respects, a misleading way. Successive editors of Swift's correspondence have resolutely ignored the fact that Swift's *Journal to Stella* is also correspondence, and should correctly be integrated with the other letters of the same period. The separate 'book' derives from Sheridan's arrangement of the correspondence, and not from Swift at all. All references in the present text are to *Jonathan Swift: Journal to Stella*, edited by Harold Williams (2 vols, Oxford, 1948).

41 The name 'Stella' is used from this point for the sake of convenience and clarity.

42 *Journal to Stella*, I, 139.

43 Ibid., p. 250. Swift carefully numbered all his letters sent to the two women in Dublin.

44 Ibid., p. 254.

45 Ibid., II, p. 409 [10 November 1711].

46 Ibid., I, p. 210.

47 Swift to Tisdall, 20 April 1704. Ball, I, p. 46.

48 Robert Harley (1661–1724), after a long and distinguished political career, became head of the Tory Ministry in 1710, firstly as Chancellor of the Exchequer, then, in 1711, as Lord Treasurer when he was raised to the peerage as Lord Oxford. His close involvement with Swift began on Swift's arrival in London, late in 1710, and their friendship continued after Harley's dismissal in 1714. His close political associate and then rival was Henry St John, later Viscount Bolingbroke.

49 A symbolic gesture which terminated State employment of high officers appointed by the Crown.

50 *Journal to Stella*, I, p. 69.

51 John Gay to Swift, 3 February 1723. Ball, III, p. 153.

52 *Journal to Stella*, I, p. 364 [20 September 1711].

53 Ibid., II, p. 662 [18 April 1713].

VI DEAN OF ST PATRICK'S
54 Vanessa to Swift, quoted in Freeman, *Vanessa and Her Corre-spondence with Jonathan Swift*, pp. 127 and 129.
55 *On the Death of Mrs Johnson*, in *Jonathan Swift: Miscellaneous and Autobiographical Pieces, Fragments and Marginalia*, edited by Herbert Davis (Oxford, 1969).
56 The Last Will and Testament of the Revd Dr Jonathan Swift (Dublin, 1984), p. 2.

Index

Figures in italic denote illustrations